DISPLACEMENT OF THE HAZARA PEOPLE OF AFGHANISTAN

Khadija Abbasi, Reza Hussaini,
Atefeh Kazemi, and Abdullah
Mohammadi

DISPLACEMENT OF
THE HAZARA PEOPLE
OF AFGHANISTAN

Complex Histories

The Forced Migration Studies
Collection

Collection Editors

T. Alexander Aleinikoff
& Laura Hammond

LPp

We dedicate this book to those who are forced to uproot from all that is familiar and who strive to construct a new homeland coloured by hope and longing.

British Library Cataloguing in Publication Data
A CIP record for this book is available from the British Library.

ISBN: 9781916985339 (pbk)
ISBN: 9781916985353 (ePDF)
ISBN: 9781916985346 (ePUB)

The right of Khadija Abbasi, Reza Hussaini, Atefeh Kazemi, Abdullah Mohammadi to be identified as the Authors of this work has been asserted by them in accordance with the Copyright, Design and Patents Act 1988.

Cover design by Fiachra McCarthy
Book design by Rachel Trolove of Twin Trail Design
Typeset by Newgen Publishing, UK

Lived Places Publishing
P.O. Box 1845
47 Echo Avenue
Miller Place, NY 11764

www.livedplacespublishing.com

Abstract

Interweaving personal narratives with critical analysis, the authors of this book highlight the complex, multidimensional experiences of forced migrants. Through the lens of the Hazara, an ethnic group with a homeland in Central Asia, we examine the emergence of informal survival networks, including smuggling networks, the ongoing racialization and exclusion of migrants seeking a homeland, the contested notion of 'return' and the challenges of navigating asylum systems in the Global North. By situating the Hazara experience within broader discussions of migration, racism, and policy, this book offers a nuanced under-standing of the intersection between forced migration, history, identity, and mobility.

Key words

Hazara, Afghanistan, Iran, UK forced displacement, exile, refugee, smuggling, return, repatriation, asylum, racism

Acknowledgements

We would like to thank our critical friend Liza Schuster, who so generously made time to listen to us and help us navigate and validate our emotions and feelings while we recalled and dug into the unpleasant memories of the past to write this book. She tirelessly encouraged us to continue. We also appreciate our peers in this volume who collectively created a safe space for us to express our thoughts and doubts. The writing of this book has been a cathartic experience and we are grateful.

Note on language

In Iran, people from Afghanistan are referred to disparagingly as *Afghani* (in Afghanistan, Afghani is used for the currency). *Afghani* has become a term of abuse by Iranians. In European languages, Afghan is used to refer to people and things from Afghanistan. Inside Afghanistan, the use of the word Afghan is very political. The government has been actively encouraging people to use the term Afghan for all citizens of Afghanistan. However, for non-Pashtun groups in Afghanistan, the term 'Afghan' is synonymous with 'Pashtun'. For many non-Pashtuns, the imposition of 'Afghans' to describe all citizens of Afghanistan is considered as a deliberate act by the governments to homogenise this country and dominate non-Pashtun identities. In response, some non-Pashtuns are arguing for a shift to 'Afghanistani', but its use is still infrequent and contested. For this reason, in spite of our discomfort, we use Afghan in this book to refer to all people from Afghanistan, but the reader should bear in mind the political, colonial, and discriminatory context in which this word is often used.

There are two national languages in Afghanistan, Dari/Farsi and Pashto, as well as several other languages. Farsi is an ancient language, used throughout the Persian empires, which included the territory of modern Afghanistan. In 1964, a political decision was taken to rename the Afghan variant of

Farsi as Dari as part of a drive to create an Afghan nation. We have decided to use Farsi as all of us grew up speaking Farsi and are attached to the work of Farsi speaking poets such as Rumi, who was born in Afghanistan.

Contents

Learning objectives

As you read through the book, we hope that you will be able to reflect on some of the ways our stories challenge the dominant narratives around forced migrants, particularly those who eventually make their way to Europe or North America.

As a first learning objective, identify at least three ways that our experiences have been shaped by social structures, including laws and policies, as well as conflict, economics, and history.

But our stories have also shown that migrants are not just passive victims of these structures—describe how we have negotiated, challenged, been defeated by, or overcome these structures.

All the authors here have experienced different migrant statuses, whether refugee, student, labour migrant, highly skilled migrant, or undocumented migrant. Critically examine the different categories into which migrants are forced, and the value and limitations of categories for those who construct them and the people to whom they are applied.

The experiences of the authors here demonstrate how racism has been interwoven into every stage of our lives, and how each different experience of forced migration exposed us to a new variation of hostility, whether based on our physical being, our perceived religion, our accent and culture, or our migration status. Articulate what you have learned about the processes of racialisation, and the link between migration and racism.

Policy is largely shaped by the three accepted durable solutions in relation to forced migrants: return, resettlement, or integration into the host community, and these describe the outcomes for many people, but do not represent a solution for all forced migrants or only following prolonged periods where none apply. Critically reflect on some of the problematic assumptions underpinning these solutions.

This book is part of a series on forced migration, and details the migrations forced upon all four of us. While inevitably, we did make choices and shaped our migration to an extent, it was definitely not freely or lightly chosen—it was often a reaction to negative events and forces. And yet, we have made the best of our experiences. Drawing on the stories below, describe the costs and benefits to migrants of migrating.

1
Introduction

Human beings have always moved, not all human beings and not all the time, but it is as natural for humans to move as it is for them to be sedentary. Looking across millennia, that movement was often driven by necessity—the need to find food, hospitable lands for crops and livestock, markets for goods, and safety from conflict and persecution. This is particularly true for the Hazara people of Afghanistan and so we hope that this book will illustrate migration experiences common to peoples across the globe. Although we consider Hazarajat, the central area of Afghanistan, our ancestral home, over centuries Hazaras have been forced to leave and to return to Afghanistan.

Mobility and immobility, both chosen and forced, are equally part of our history, a history that is only now being written, and written by Hazara scholars. This is important as, until recently, the history of Afghanistan has been written either by non-Afghans or by dominant groups in Afghanistan that do not include the Hazara. For us, this book is an act of resistance to the discrimination we face. Migration is not just the act of a victim—it is people deciding to resist racialization and victimisation by seeking out places where they can achieve their full potential.

The authors of this book are Afghan scholars who have experienced migration and exile. We are all Hazara and have all grown up in Iran. **Atefeh Kazemi** is a PhD student in anthropology at McGill University, Montreal; **Khadija Abbasi** is a Teaching Fellow at SOAS, and currently in Manila and wrote her PhD at the Geneva Graduate Institute on the experiences of young transnational Hazaras; **Reza Hussaini** is a researcher, currently doing his PhD at City, University of London, but now in Sacramento; **Abdullah Mohammadi** is an M.A. graduate in Demography from the University of Tehran and currently works for the Mixed Migration Centre, and lives in Stockholm. Khadija has been through the UK asylum system, was granted refugee status, and now has British citizenship. Abdullah and Reza were evacuated from Kabul in August 2021. Reza and his family went first to Poland before being brought to the UK as he had a student visa. They then moved to the US. Atefeh was the last to leave Iran in August 2024.

We belong to a small but growing community of Hazara scholars who are adapting to academia in exile. Within this community, working across a range of disciplines and on a wide variety of topics, a subcommunity is focused on analysing the experiences and history of our people, and as we will show, migration plays a central role in that history. Although belonging to a minority that has experienced discrimination and persecution, and having experienced racism ourselves, we recognize that we four are privileged. Most Hazaras, including our parents, have not had access to higher education or white-collar jobs. Fewer still have managed to travel beyond the countries neighbouring Afghanistan. Our upward social mobility is recent, and we have all either shared or witnessed the restrictions experienced by those who have not had our opportunities.

Many Hazaras are migrants by birth, born in exile but with no access to the citizenship of our birthplaces when those birthplaces are Iran or Pakistan, condemned to die as migrants even if we never leave those countries. We have been labour migrants for decades, often highly skilled but condemned to unskilled labour. We have moved back and forth across neighbouring borders, shifting between legal and social categories—each of us writing here has been at different times, (and sometimes simultaneously) students, workers, refugees, asylum seekers, undocumented migrants, or returned migrants. We have 'returned' to Afghanistan but been unable to return to our village or province, and so remain displaced within Afghanistan.

The stories here illustrate this complexity. They overlap in places as we share some similar experiences. In the rest of this chapter, we provide the context and history necessary to understand each of the stories.

History of Hazara migration

Today, the Hazara can be found in many Afghan provinces, and there are significant populations of Hazaras in Kabul, Herat, and Mazar, but our homeland is regarded as Hazarajat in central Afghanistan. Hazarajat today includes the provinces of Bamiyan and Daikundi, and several adjacent districts in the provinces of Ghazni, Uruzgan, Wardak, Parwan, Baghlan, Samangan and Sar-e Pul. Migration has long been a survival strategy for Afghans (Monsutti, 2005), including Hazaras, though there is also a population of Hazaras, especially in rural areas of Afghanistan like Bamiyan, who have never moved. But all of us, within our family circles, have relatives who have left the country, in most cases due to poverty or persecution, and more recently, prolonged drought in Hazarajat drove thousands to leave for the cities. To understand the forced migration of the Hazaras, we outline the history of Hazaras in Afghan society, which has been a history of persecution, flight and resistance. This history shows clearly that academic categories cannot capture the complexity of forced migration.

There is no **majority** ethnic group in Afghanistan, but the largest **minority** groups are the Pashtuns, Tajiks, Uzbeks, and Hazaras. There has not been a complete census in Afghanistan since 1979, so we only have rough estimates of a population that has been marked by high birth rates, high mortality, and high migration. There are different estimates that suggest the Pashtuns make

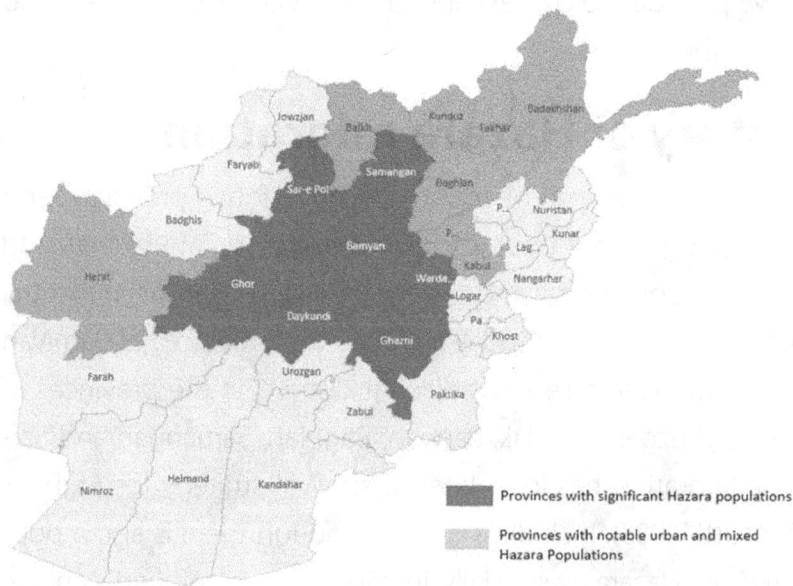

Figure 1.1 Map of Afghanistan showing provinces, ethnic spread and neighbouring states

up 40–47 per cent of the population, Tajiks 12–27 per cent, and Uzbeks approximately 9 per cent, with other ethnicities, such as Turkmen, Aimak, and Balouch, each accounting for less than 5 per cent. Today, the Hazaras make up about 20 per cent of the population of Afghanistan but before the genocide, (see below) we were the largest ethnic group in Afghanistan (Mousavi, 2018). These populations are not spread evenly across the country, and some provinces are dominated by one ethnic group. In our case, these were the central provinces of Afghanistan, but as we show below, our position in Hazarajat has been undermined.

Hazaras are physically distinct from Afghanistan's other ethnic groups (though we are physically similar to Uzbeks and Turkmen), with features more usually found in East Asia. We are often racialized based on our physiognomy, which makes it easy to identify and target us, not just in Afghanistan, but also in Iran and Pakistan where most Hazaras have sought refuge. We have often been subjected to racialized mockery and stereotyping, including derogatory remarks about our physical appearance or perceived differences in cultural practices, which have served to marginalize and dehumanize us. Khadija was once asked by a classmate if she could see well with her 'narrow' eyes. Our physical features have been intertwined with racial assumptions made about us—that we are fit only for physical labour, that we are incapable of intellectual labour, and undeserving of autonomy and power, such that Hazaras in Afghanistan, Iran, and Pakistan are treated differently. This racialization, and the racism it engenders and justifies, is a theme that we explore below and in our individual chapters. Schuster (2010) has argued that migration and racism are intimately linked, and our experience is a testament to that linkage.

Most other ethnic groups, including the dominant Pashtuns, belong to the Sunni branch of Islam, while Hazaras are Shia, and considered *Rafizi* (heretics), an accusation used even today to justify our persecution in Afghanistan. A minority of Hazaras belong to the Ismaili sect, and some are Sunni, but whatever our religion, we stand out physically and are easy targets. However, the precarious position occupied by the Hazaras today can be traced back to the actions of one person in particular. In the nineteenth century, we accounted for nearly two-thirds of the population (Minority Rights Group International, 2008). There had been earlier tensions between Hazaras and Pashtuns; then with the approval and support of the British government, Abdur Rahman Khan (1880–1901), ruler of Afghanistan, set out to Pashtunise Afghanistan by confiscating land from non-Pashtuns and settling Pashtuns across the country (Bleuer, 2012).

As noted by Bleuer, 'since Abdur Rahman's rise to power, almost every Afghan ruler until 1979 had a policy of attempting to "homogenise" the peoples of Afghanistan. As part of this process …[of] "Pashtunisation," the Afghan government used Pashtun nationalist ideology, land confiscation, discriminatory taxation policies, and forced resettlement that favoured the Pashtuns' (2012, 70). Abdur Rahman Khan moved all ethnic groups, including Pashtuns, around the country to consolidate his power and create Pashtun domination in strategic areas. In Hazarajat, parts of which had been independent, this Pashtunising policy alongside heavy taxes, sectarian conflict, corruption, and violence of the government forces led to a rebellion in 1892.

Abdur Rahman Khan declared jihad against the Shias and sent a large army (supported by British military advisers) to put down the rebellion. They captured Urozgān, where the rebellion originated, and massacred the local population: 'thousands of Hazara men, women, and children were sold as slaves in the markets of Kabul and Qandahar, while numerous towers of human heads were made from the defeated rebels as a warning to others who might challenge the rule of the Amir' (Mousavi, 1998, cited by Monsutti, 2003). Between 1888 and 1893, more than half of the Hazara population was massacred or fled to neighbouring countries and farther afield and their lands were confiscated, and distributed among non-Hazaras (Mousavi, 2018; Ibrahimi, 2017). The memory of these events and the massacres that have followed, which amounted to a genocide, are a source of ongoing trauma for the Hazara people. It has coloured our relationship with a Pashtun-dominated Afghan state that has continued to single us out for harassment and persecution, even as relations with individual members of the dominant minorities have sometimes been supportive and warm.

When distinctions are made between political refugees and economic or labour migrants, it is important to understand that such distinctions do not make sense for Hazaras (and many other groups) when discrimination and persecution have economic consequences. The poverty driving Hazaras to seek work in Iran was a direct result of discrimination and persecution. The grant of Hazara lands to Pashtun nomads by Abdur Rahman Khan meant that the Hazaras who stayed often became tenants on their own land. Later, attempts were made to impose discriminatory taxes on Hazaras. Both of these strategies have returned under the second Taliban regime. The enforced impoverishment of Hazara people obliged many to become seasonal migrants to Kabul, Herat, and Mazar, and to Mashhad in Iran and Quetta in Pakistan. Hazaras worked as day labourers in construction or as porters in the markets, where once again racialization by the host states and societies confined us to particular areas and occupations, as Atefeh shows in Chapter 3. Refugees need to work to survive and support their families, but this is often used as an excuse to label us economic migrants, thereby exempting us from the protection that refugee status might afford us (Schuster, 2016).

The communist era 1979–1989

The forced displacement of Hazaras (and other Afghans) accelerated first due to the severe drought of 1978, and then the Soviet intervention in 1979, which led to a decade of conflict between the Soviet forces and the Afghan resistance fighters or *Mujahedin* (Kakar 1995). We Hazaras are not a homogeneous group; some of us supported the communist government and others the *Mujahedin*. Much of the fighting in Hazarajat was between different Hazara groups (Ibrahimi, 2017). In June 1979, following an unarmed uprising by Shia in the Chindawol area of Kabul, the Communist government launched an attack. Over two days, many were killed, while others were taken away and their deaths were only confirmed by a Dutch War Crimes Investigation years later in 2012.

It is estimated that 1.5 million Afghans died in that decade and millions fled to Iran and Pakistan, though a few found their way to other countries, including Britain and Germany. Hazaras mostly fled to places with already existing Hazara communities, such as Mashhad in Iran and Quetta in Pakistan. Up until this point, migration outside the country had mostly been by men, with families left behind in Afghanistan (Hussaini et al., 2021). But the war between the Soviets and the *Mujahedin* saw whole families, and in some cases villages, displaced. Although Hazaratown, a Hazara ghetto in Quetta, expanded at this time, at least half of those Afghans who went to Pakistan were confined to refugee camps, especially around Peshawar.

In Iran, the situation was different. Ayatollah Khomeini, who had just taken over leadership of Iran, welcomed Shia refugees from the Soviet occupiers as *Muhajir*, religious refugees fleeing what was seen as a Soviet attack on Islamic ways of life. However, although some Afghans in Iran are recognised as refugees by UNHCR, the Iranian Republic has never recognised us as refugees according to the 1951 Convention, to which it is a signatory. The concept of *Hijrat* initially ensured that as Shias in Iran we could rely on the religious duties of our hosts to protect those who had fled for religious reasons (Safri, 2011). As noted by Safri, 'by describing the Afghans as refugees who struggled to maintain religious faith in the face of a Soviet campaign seeking its eradication, both Pakistan and Iran simultaneously positioned themselves as performing a righteous function' (2011: 589). Although Iran had signed the Geneva Convention and the New York Protocol, the government chose to designate Afghans as *Muhajir*, rather than refugees, giving them Blue Cards (identity cards).

Most Iranian scholars (Adelkhah and Olszewska, 2007; Abbasi-Shavazi et al., 2008; Vossughi and Mohseni, 2016) emphasise the generous welcome given to Afghan refugees, citing the words of Ayatollah Khomeini 'Islam has no borders', the social benefits Afghans were allowed to access, such as subsidised health care and free primary and secondary education, and the economic costs to the state: 1.5 million refugees, mostly Hazaras, were allowed to settle in Iranian cities, including Tehran, Mashhad, Isfahan, and Qom, though since then the number of zones forbidden to us has increased to 16 provinces, and many cities. The restrictions imposed on us within cities have trapped us in ghettos such as Golshahr in Mashhad, Pakdasht in Tehran, Shahr Qaem in Qom, or Zeinabiyye in Isfahan. In the third chapter, Atefeh focuses on the collective experience of Hazara youth growing up in Golshahr, most of whom are Iran-born, and explores how they perceive themselves as *muhajirs* in Iran, where the term '*muhajir*' was stripped of its initial religious connotation by the 1990s.

Hazaras growing up in Iran emphasise the economic contribution we made to different sectors, which explains that early welcome. The discovery of oil in Iran (and in the Gulf States) created a massive demand for labour, in particular manual labour (Safri, 2011). Safri (2011) and Monsutti (2008) both point out that Afghans had to apply for work permits that only allowed them to work in mines, brick factories, and construction. We responded to labour shortages because we were not confined to camps but were self-settled around the country, often following the demand for labour. Although economic changes in Iran led to an economic downturn and increased unemployment, Hazara men were welcomed into the army, where we fought alongside Iranians in the Iran-Iraq war (1980–1988).

However, the withdrawal of Soviet forces from Afghanistan in 1989 and the collapse of the Soviet Union, together with the death of Ayatollah Khomeini, saw a shift in the attitude of the Iranian government towards Afghan refugees. There were posters in Afghan neighbourhoods telling us it was time to go 'home'. The pressure increased as the 1990–1991 Gulf War sent a quarter of the Iraqi population across the border to Iran. Iran was hosting 3 million Afghan and 1.5 million Iraqi refugees, who were less visible than we Hazaras. But it had become impossible for most of us to return to Afghanistan (approximately 600,000 Afghans, not all Hazaras, did return), not least because of the civil war that erupted.

Civil war

Following the removal of Najibullah, the Communist president of Afghanistan, civil war broke out in 1992. After the *Mujahidin* (resistance fighters) took power that year, fighting between the different factions broke out. Violent attacks occurred in Kabul between the different forces, killing many Hazaras, including unarmed civilians, and many Hazara women were raped (Ahmad). In February 1993, hundreds of Hazara residents in the Afshar district of West Kabul were massacred by government forces under the direction of Burhanuddin Rabbani and Ahmed Shah Massoud, joined by Abdul Rasul Sayyaf and his *Ittehad-i-Islami* group. The fighting saw the utter devastation of large areas of Kabul, particularly those inhabited by Hazaras (Afghanistan Justice Report 2005).

Once again, Afghanistan saw the displacement of millions of people, much of it internal, but significant numbers migrating once again to Iran and Pakistan, while some made longer journeys to Europe, Australia, and the US. We also learned at this time that it was not only our neighbours who did not want us—Europe's asylum policies were becoming more restrictive and new laws were introduced in Britain and Germany.

The Taliban 1993–2001

In spite of factors causing continued displacement within and from Afghanistan, host states increased the pressure on refugees to return. At the same time, during a period of increased unemployment in Iran, the Blue Cards were declared invalid and there was a shift from the term *Muhajir* to that of *Awaregan* (displaced person), which did not have the same positive connotation.

According to Safri (2011: 593), 1.3 million Afghans were repatriated from Iran between 1992 and 1995, despite continuing conflict and insecurity in Afghanistan. This coincided with a more general shift in the mid-1990s, including by UNHCR, from

Figure 1.2 Khadija's Blue Card on which the diagonal line says: The identification card for the Afghan Awaragan

a preference for resettling refugees to one of repatriation, and it was no longer necessary for that repatriation to be voluntary (Chimni, 2004). Instead, it was now the state's right to decide whether it was safe enough to return refugees to their state of origin. As Chimni points out, states from the Global North had no grounds to criticise states such as Iran or Pakistan who were hosting and repatriating many more refugees than they were, but there was little evidence that they were against this policy, even as more Afghans were leaving in response to the brutality of the Taliban regime (Langenkampf, 2003). The shift towards temporary protection and to keeping refugees in their regions, as well as to 'imposed return' (abandoning the 'voluntary' element), had serious implications for Afghans, especially after the fall of the Taliban. From this time on, it became extremely difficult for people to seek asylum in the Global North without the help of smugglers, as Abdullah describes in Chapter 2.

The republic 2001–2021

The period following the fall of the Taliban regime saw massive changes in Afghanistan: the arrival of foreign armies, thousands of aid workers and NGOs, new opportunities, a continuing conflict, and ebbs and flows of migration in and out of the country. New opportunities, such as access to education and different, more skilled employment opportunities arose for Hazara people. We became increasingly visible as business people, parliamentarians, civil society activists, and in the media. However, we were still subject to discrimination as described by Reza in Chapter 4 and Khadija in Chapter 5 and had often to set up our own schools, universities, businesses, and media companies. For those of us who travelled to Afghanistan from Iran hoping to find a home and end our exile, it was a shock to see how Hazaras were treated in our *watan*, our homeland. We found ourselves discriminated against not just because of our physical appearance and religion, but because we came with Iranian accents and manners.

Immediately after the US attacks in December 2001, the borders of Afghanistan had been sealed by its neighbours, so that the number of refugees was relatively low—about 200,000—while the number of IDPs soared from 1.2 to 2 million. Most IDPs were in poorly serviced camps, with little access to food or medical support and with no institutional protector similar to UNHCR for refugees (Cohen, 2002). Adding to the IDP population were returnees. Safri (2011) points out that very quickly Afghans were expected to 'return' to Afghanistan and those who remained in Iran and Pakistan after the fall of the Taliban were reconstructed as 'labour' or 'undocumented' migrants instead of refugees. Afghans returned rapidly from Iran and Pakistan—too rapidly according to UNHCR, so that in 2002, the new government was completely overwhelmed, and the country was unable to cope. Within the first two years, more than 5 million people had returned to Afghanistan, but most were unable to return to their homes in rural areas—approximately 50 per cent settled in and around Kabul.

Afghanistan continued to experience instability and insecurity. In December 2009, Obama tried to break the stalemate by ordering a surge in the number of troops, but two years later began to reduce the numbers significantly. 2014 was a difficult year. With the reduction in foreign troops, insecurity had worsened, not helped by the inconclusive presidential elections. US Senator

John Kerry visited Kabul and negotiated a power-sharing government with Ashraf Ghani as President and his rival Abdullah Abdullah as Chief Executive of the government. However, negotiations between the two over who would allocate which Ministry contributed to ongoing instability. This had an impact on security and saw international companies and NGOs withdrawing from Afghanistan, which in turn weakened the economy, increased unemployment, and strengthened the Taliban. This period saw increased attacks and casualties.

Internationally, war in Syria was driving millions of refugees northwards, mostly to Jordan, Lebanon, and Turkey, but also to Europe. When Angela Merkel responded by saying that these arrivals were manageable, Afghans who had found life more and more difficult in neighboring countries sought solutions outside the region. However, Europe's warm welcome was short-lived, and the reception quickly turned hostile. In March 2016, the EU signed a deal with Turkey, according to which Turkey agreed to prevent Syrians and Afghans from travelling on to Europe in exchange for 3 billion euros in aid and easier access to the EU for Turkish citizens. A few months later, the EU succeeded in bullying the Afghan government into signing the Joint Way Forward by threatening to withhold 1.5 billion euros in development aid (Hussaini and Schuster, 2022). To access the aid, the Afghan government was forced to agree to accept forced returns and prevent 'illegal' migration.

The second coming of the Taliban

In 2017, a new President, Donald Trump, took office in the US and began negotiating with the Taliban, and in February 2020, the US and the Taliban announced the Doha Agreement, under which the US agreed to withdraw all U.S. forces from Afghanistan by May 2021. By the time Biden took office in January 2021 and confirmed the withdrawal of the remaining 2,500 troops, the Taliban were already in control of half of Afghanistan. It was assumed that the Afghanistan National Defence and Security Forces (ANDSF) would take over responsibility for security, though in reality, it was acknowledged that the Taliban would probably re-take power within a year of withdrawal. Instead, they swept back into power in August, entering Kabul on Sunday, August 15, 2021.

The shock in the capital was profound. In the days before their arrival, people were flooding into the city, ATMs were emptied, and the skies were filled with the clatter of helicopters as foreigners fled. The day the Taliban arrived, tens of thousands of people gathered at the airport hoping to flee. In Chapter 4, Reza describes the trauma of those days. The evacuation was officially completed by the end of August, and people could no longer leave by air.

For those left behind, the situation deteriorated rapidly. Our habitual destinations of Iran and Pakistan closed their borders. The Hazara community, already marginalised and persecuted, faced heightened threats under the Taliban regime. The Taliban's history of targeting Hazaras for their ethnic and religious identity raised immediate concerns for their safety. As a result, thousands of Hazaras sought refuge in neighbouring countries, primarily Iran and Pakistan, despite the closed borders and perilous journeys. Checkpoints multiplied, and at each one, we were required to hand over bribes, cash, jewellery, or some other valuables.

Beatings and sexual harassment were commonplace. The desperation of those fleeing persecution and economic collapse led to significant numbers of undocumented crossings. By early 2022, it was estimated that around 300,000 Afghans, including a large proportion of Hazaras, had fled to Iran. In Pakistan, the influx was smaller but still substantial, with thousands of Hazaras seeking refuge, particularly in areas with existing Hazara communities such as Quetta. Despite mass deportations from those countries, people continue to cross into Iran and Pakistan, driven as much by the collapsing economy as the gender apartheid of the Taliban regime. Once again, we find ourselves in precarious and unstable situations, fearing deportation and fearful for those left behind.

This new phase of displacement of Hazaras, driven by both the immediate threat of violence and the broader economic collapse under the Taliban regime, is a continuation of a long history of forced migration and persecution. The new Taliban regime has done nothing to assure the protection of marginalised groups, and reports of targeted attacks against Hazaras continue to surface.

For the Hazaras who managed to evacuate to Western countries, the challenges are different. Many face difficulties in navigating asylum systems, securing stable housing and employment, and dealing with the psychological trauma of their sudden displacement and the loss of their homeland. Additionally, there is a deep sense of survivor's guilt among those who have reached safety, coupled with a profound concern for family and friends left behind.

The consequences of migration

Migration is a norm for many Hazaras, who share experiences of migration for survival, security, marriage, labour and education, and often for a combination of all of these reasons (Monsutti, 2005). It is often seen as a necessary and normal, though painful, experience for both the migrant and those left behind (Aranda, 2007). The impact of migration on Hazaras, individually and collectively, in Afghanistan and in exile has been profound and multi-faceted, impacting every aspect of life from economic opportunities to cultural identities.

While structural barriers, discriminatory policies and limited opportunities in Afghanistan have historically restricted Hazaras to low-paying, unskilled labour, migration has often been the only avenue to escape poverty and provide for families. In host countries like Iran and Pakistan, as well as further afield in Europe and Australia, Hazara migrants frequently take on labour-intensive jobs that local populations are unwilling to perform. While these jobs are often exploitative and low-paying, they offer a lifeline to those who would otherwise face destitution. In countries with more supportive refugee policies, such as in parts of Europe and Australia, Hazara migrants have been able to access education and higher-paying jobs, contributing significantly to their host economies. The remittances sent back home are vital for the survival of families in Afghanistan, where economic opportunities remain scarce. Monsutti (2012) in his book, *War and Migration*, explains the role of migration and remittances as a survival strategy among Hazaras.

Migration has also deeply affected the social and cultural fabric of the Hazara communities. In host countries, Hazara communities have often formed tight-knit diasporas, maintaining cultural practices and languages while adapting to new environments. These diasporas provide crucial social support networks, helping new arrivals navigate the challenges of settling in a new country. However, migration can also lead to cultural dilution and identity challenges. Younger generations born in host countries may struggle with dual identities, balancing the cultural expectations of their parents with the norms of the society they are growing up in. In Afghanistan, many of the second-generation born in exile have experienced discrimination upon return due to their distinct behaviours and values adopted from host countries. Despite these challenges, the Hazara diaspora has managed to preserve a strong sense of identity and community. Cultural organisations and religious centres play a vital role in this preservation. Literature also plays an important role here.

The psychological toll of forced migration on the Hazaras, especially among those evacuated in August 2021, cannot be overstated. The trauma of displacement, the experience of violence and persecution, and the constant fear for the safety of family members left behind contribute to high levels of stress and mental health issues among Hazara refugees. For those who arrived in host countries via irregular journeys, the uncertainty of asylum processes and the threat of deportation add to this burden.

As explained above, survivor's guilt is also a common experience among those who were evacuated from Kabul airport in

August 2021. The relief of being safe is often accompanied by a deep sense of guilt for those left behind, exacerbated by the dire conditions in Afghanistan under Taliban rule. Many Hazara refugees also face discrimination and racism in host countries, namely, Iran and Pakistan, compounding their sense of isolation and marginalisation.

Another prominent consequence of migration among Hazaras has been the increased political engagement of their diaspora, especially in countries with established communities. Hazara migrants and refugees have become advocates for human rights, both in Afghanistan and in their host countries. For example, we have witnessed different communities of Hazaras in European states reaching out to lobby states and parliamentarians, forming advocacy groups, and raising international awareness about the plight of the Hazara people in Afghanistan. While in the current situation within Afghanistan, Hazaras are almost completely deprived of their political rights, we are expecting that the Hazara diaspora will play a crucial role in shaping political discourse in the future.

And, finally, access to education has been one of the most transformative aspects of migration for the Hazara community. In host countries, Hazara children and young adults have had opportunities that would have been unimaginable in Afghanistan. This access to education has empowered a new generation of Hazara scholars, professionals, and activists who are contributing to their communities and beyond. For many Hazaras, education is seen as the key to breaking the cycle of poverty and discrimination.

Structure of the book

These are the histories of individuals and are not representative of the whole Hazara population—not all use smugglers, not everyone returned or wanted to return, the experiences of Hazaras in Iran differed in degree from those in Pakistan, people experienced more or less discrimination, the experience of Afghanistan was not the same for everyone who left Iran, and the journey to the West was also very different for different people.

The following four chapters address different aspects of the Hazara migration experience. Abdullah tells the story of his cousin, a guide who helps Hazaras to leave Afghanistan for Iran and Pakistan, challenging the dominant narratives of smugglers. Smugglers may be criminals, exploiting the desperation and vulnerability of those forced to flee, but those smugglers are a product of increasingly restrictive policies that seek to impose immobility, especially on poor populations. But historically in Afghanistan, *Rahbalad* (guides) were used to assist those who needed to move to find a place of safety and, as such, treated with respect. This chapter explains the important role people like Abdullah's cousin play for Hazara migrants.

Atefeh describes growing up as a migrant in the Golshahr area of Mashhad, Iran. For Atefeh and her generation, Golshahr is where the duality of being born and socialised in Iran and being excluded as a *muhajir* is deeply interwoven with narratives of hope, hopelessness, and struggles for survival and resilience. She describes how Golshahr was both a source of safety and restriction and what it was like as a Hazara woman to venture out into mainstream Iranian society, and the humiliation and rejection she experienced. In this chapter, she refers to the attempts of young Hazaras to resist racialisation, to insist on their right to be more than unskilled labourers.

At different points, Afghans were encouraged to leave Iran and 'return' to Afghanistan, especially after the fall of the Taliban in 2001, even though they may have been born or raised in Iran and never left Iran. As Reza explains, those making this journey to a country at once familiar and alien did so with a mixture of hope and trepidation, and this often led to bitter disappointment and disillusionment. While in Iran, we were singled out because of how we look—unlike Pashtuns or Tajiks, we did not blend in and were referred to disparagingly as *Afghani*. Now in Afghanistan, we were mocked for our Iranian accents, dress, and manners and referred to as '*Iranigak*', i.e., little Iranians. For many of us, it became clear that to have a future, we needed to move further away.

Although Khadija had done a master's degree in the UK before she decided to return to ask for asylum, the reaction to her change of status as well as the torture of the asylum process and detention was a profound shock. In Chapter 5, Khadija explains why she made her claim, her asylum journey, and what it was like to find herself in a third exile, where this time hostility and discrimination are tied to the legal status of being an asylum seeker.

The final chapter draws out the lessons to be learnt from these different stories, lessons that can be applied to other groups of displaced people in different contexts, before we suggest some small projects that you might undertake.

2
A smuggler's story: Survival and necessity in Afghan migration

Abdullah Mohammadi

The first time I met Saber[1] was in our house when I was around 17 or 18 years old, living with my parents in Qom, Iran. Saber was a young man, around 21 or 22 years old, dressed in typical Afghan attire, and just arrived from Afghanistan. He was supposed to stay at our house for a couple of weeks. I remember those two weeks very well; our house became the centre of family gatherings, and people, both relatives and strangers, came and went from early morning until late at night. Saber was at the heart of these gatherings, continuously talking, shaking hands, laughing, and again talking and talking and talking. Despite his youth, everyone spoke to him with respect, even the elderly, addressing him as 'Saber Khan'! One day, someone knocked on the door. When I opened it, I saw a man and a woman waiting impatiently in the winter cold outside. The man said, 'We've come to see *Saber-e Rahbalad* (Saber, the Guide).' It was the first time I heard the word *Rahbalad*, and I didn't understand its meaning. So, with an obvious hesitation in my tone, I invited them in. From that day on, Saber's presence would be felt with friends, relatives, and strangers coming to our house for a couple of weeks every two or three years. As I grew older, I learned that Saber's job was to bring people from Afghanistan to Iran and take back goods, merchandise, and letters to Afghanistan. However, he was no longer a *Rahbalad*—people now called him a *Qachaqbar* (smuggler).

Some years later, during those years, when Afghan refugee youth in Iran were not allowed to attend high school and university, I left Iran for Afghanistan. Tired of the gruelling life with no prospect for the future, I, who had never stepped outside of Qom until then, took a leap of faith and decided to go to Afghanistan, to my father's homeland, hoping I could create a different future for myself.

First I went to Mashhad and, after staying with one of my cousins for a few days, I introduced myself to the police at the Chahar Cheshmeh camp as an undocumented individual intending to return to Afghanistan. I stayed at the camp for a week until one Saturday, along with about two hundred other Afghans, I was sent to the Islam Qala border. When I crossed the border, I walked with the crowd towards the taxis heading to Herat, but before I reached the station, someone called my name. I turned around and saw Saber smiling and approaching me. He greeted me, hugged me, and simply said, 'Welcome, *Bola Jan* (dear cousin)!' He then explained that the other cousin in Mashhad had informed him in advance that I had introduced myself to the police and would soon be deported to a country I had never seen before. Apparently, he had been coming to the border to find me every

day for a week between 2 and 5 PM, the time when the depor-
tees were crossing the border. I found him still cheerful, talkative,
and full of life. I was his guest for three days before going to Kabul.

A year after my arrival in Kabul, a family emergency arose in Qom,
necessitating my return to Iran. Despite my efforts, I was unable
to obtain an Iranian visa through official channels. I contacted
Saber and explained my predicament, to which he responded
with calm assurance: 'Don't worry, Bola Jan. If you come to Herat
by this Friday, I'll take you back to your parents by the next Friday.'
Thus, my journey from Herat to Qom was facilitated by *Saber-e
Qachaqbar*. This journey, along with subsequent meetings with
Saber over the years, provided me with insights into his life and
profession. These interactions allowed me to engage with other
smugglers and understand the broader context of their activities. In 2016, after completing my university education, I joined
a research institute focusing on the Afghan displacement experience. Since then, the smuggling of migrants has remained a
central area of my focus. In this chapter, I will recount some of
the conversations I had with Saber, exploring how he became a
smuggler. Additionally, I will present some observations on the
dynamics of migrant smuggling within the Afghan context.

Smuggling of migrants in Afghanistan

Afghanistan has a long tradition of movement and migration,
highlighting how Afghan populations have historically utilised
migration in various forms (Klaus, 2006). Nomads move to access
better pasturelands, businessmen migrate for trade, and pilgrims

travel to religious sites, both Shia and Sunni. Migration, in addition, has long served as a survival strategy for Afghans (Monsutti, 2008), particularly during times of crisis. This is especially evident in the country's recent history, marked by decades of war, political instability, and economic hardship. Over the past 40 years, many Afghans have sought refuge in neighbouring countries like Pakistan and Iran and farther afield in Europe and Australia. The large-scale displacement began with the Soviet invasion in 1979 and continued through the civil wars of the 1990s and the rise of the Taliban. Each phase of conflict and instability has pushed more Afghans to migrate in search of safety and better opportunities. However, challenges in accessing regular migration pathways have persisted. Securing visas is often difficult and costly, involving significant bureaucratic hurdles. These barriers, combined with the pressing need to escape deteriorating conditions, have made Afghanistan a lucrative market for smuggling networks. Smugglers provide services such as transportation, shelter, and assistance in crossing borders. Their role has become so ingrained in the Afghan migration culture that they are often seen as more than just service providers. In many cases, smugglers adopt the persona of saviours, essential figures who facilitate the possibility of finding refuge and a new life in a safe place (Mohammadi et al., 2019).

Smuggling also has deep historical roots in Afghanistan, linked to traditional forms of migration for pilgrimage, trade, and education. Nomads, traders, and pilgrims have long relied on guides or *Rahbalads*, whose role extended beyond simple navigation; they were responsible for the safety and well-being of those they led. This tradition has carried over into the modern context of migrant smuggling, where individuals like Saber see themselves as continuing a legacy of providing critical assistance in times of need. In fact, the last four decades of political and economic instability have just reinforced the role of smugglers.

Over the last six years, I spoke to many Afghan smugglers in Zaranj, Herat, Kandahar, and Kabul and what I observed is that while the official narrative might associate smuggling with 'illegality' and 'exploitation', within Afghan society, there is often a more nuanced understanding of this phenomenon. Terms like *Rahbalad* (guide) carry positive connotations, referring to those who help people in desperate times. Similarly, the term *Qachaqbar* (smuggler) is used in a relatively neutral manner, devoid of the heavily negative implications it might have elsewhere (Majidi, 2018). This linguistic nuance reflects a broader cultural acceptance of the role smugglers play in Afghan society. Many Afghan smugglers see themselves as providing a necessary service that the government fails to offer. They argue that in the absence of state support and amid widespread corruption, their work is essential for helping people escape dire circumstances. This self-perception is shared by Afghan communities, who view smugglers not as criminals but as practical solutions to a failing system. The story of *Saber-e Qachaqbar* is a good example.

Becoming a smuggler: Saber's story

A messenger

Following the withdrawal of Soviet forces from Afghanistan in 1989 and the start of conflicts among various jihadist groups, a civil war erupted throughout the country. Different parties gained control over different zones, mostly along ethnic lines. A similar situation prevailed in some major cities. For instance, in 1992, after the fall of Najibullah's government, different political groups poured into Kabul, each seizing control of a part of the city. Kabul turned into a segmented city controlled by different political parties organised along ethnic lines: Pashtun, Tajik, Uzbek and Hazara.

One of the first consequences of this territorialization was the movement restrictions imposed by different parties. If someone intended to travel, for example, from Bamiyan to Kabul, a distance of 180km, they had to obtain passage permits from at least three parties. For those who wanted to travel farther and leave the country for any reason, it was very challenging to get all the permits, so *Rahbalads* provided an essential service. Many Hazara, often travelling in groups, relied on these *Rahbalads*. They were more than just guides; they were lifelines in a war-torn country where official pathways were blocked or too dangerous.

According to Saber, *Rahbalads* were primarily individuals involved in trade, accompanying their caravans of pilgrims and travellers to neighbouring countries. Their role extended beyond mere guidance; they were leaders of caravans, responsible for the safety and well-being of the people travelling with them on risky paths.

During this period, Saber and his family were living in Bamiyan. His father was originally a trader and one of the local *Rahbalads*, someone who from an early age travelled frequently to Kabul, bringing goods and food supplies to Bamiyan. Alongside domestic travels, he also travelled to Pakistan and Iran for trade and had a shop in Quetta.

> My father usually travelled every year between Bamiyan, Kabul, and Quetta, and sometimes twice a year. He had a car and would take local products, such as butter, *qurut* (dried cheese), rugs, and skins from Bamiyan to Kabul. He also transported patients to Kabul for medical treatment. After Kabul, he would load up with other goods and head across the border with Pakistan towards Quetta.

Alongside his business, Saber's father was involved in political activities and had connections with *Hizb-e Wahdat*, the Hazara political group that controlled Bamiyan and the west of Kabul at that time. Almost all political parties and factions had offices not only in Afghanistan but in Pakistan and Iran as well. These offices served as representatives for Afghan migrants in those countries and as political liaisons with host country authorities. However, due to the lack of communication networks at that time, communication between these offices was not straightforward, and messages and letters were carried and circulated by individuals. These letters were not given to just anyone. Due to potential risks and sensitive information, only trusted individuals could carry these messages.

Saber's father was one of those trusted individuals. Saber remembers how his father used to deliver letters on some of his journeys to Quetta. His father even took him along sometimes since the presence of a child made them less suspicious:

> He sometimes took me with him on these journeys, and I would see that in Kabul, before heading to Quetta, he

spent 2–3 days visiting relatives and acquaintances, and some other individuals. During these visits, some letters with addresses were given to my father, which he took with him to Quetta and delivered to their acquaintances. Later, I found out that some of those letters were political letters that my father brought from Bamiyan and Kabul to Quetta.

The return journeys were similar, with many letters entrusted to his father, not only political letters but also letters from relatives, friends, and strangers who wanted to send messages to their loved ones in Afghanistan. This letter delivery was almost a regular and routine practice since at that time there were no phones or computers that allowed everyone to contact their family and loved ones within minutes.

Accompanying his father on journeys gradually acquainted Saber with the intricacies of trade and travel. He learned that products like dairy products, edible oil, and rugs from Bamiyan had many customers in Kabul. Additionally, items like skins, carpets, and dried fruits from Kabul sold well in Quetta. Bringing home appliances, batteries, textiles, as well as certain food supplies from Quetta to Kabul and Bamiyan proved to be lucrative for them. Saber also became well-acquainted with the routes; he learned where to stop at nights, where they expected to face a checkpoint, what to say at various checkpoints, to whom they should give bribes or what permits to show at each checkpoint, and how to conceal letters:

When we had sensitive letters, it wasn't just writing them on paper and maybe hiding them in a pocket or inside the vehicle. If someone at a checkpoint became suspicious and wanted to interrogate us, then they would turn the entire vehicle upside down and search all our pockets. So one thing that my father sometimes did was to write very sensitive letters on a piece of cloth, tying it around my waist. Once they even wrote a letter on the undershirt I was wearing. I was a teenager, and rarely did someone touch a teenager like me, especially in the presence of my father.

During these journeys, Saber noticed the respect people had for his father. This respect wasn't just due to his relative prosperity but also because of his role in connecting separated families and people—acting as a bridge between two worlds. He was a kind of messenger:

Everyone loved my father. Whenever we were in Kabul or Quetta, mornings, afternoons, and evenings were filled with invitations. My father was highly esteemed. People knew that he was risking his life for them.

Gradually, Saber realised that he, too, had a share in this respect, and people looked at him differently. No one treated him like an ordinary teenager, and they addressed him as 'Agha Saber (Mr. Saber).' However, these journeys were not easy for a teenager. Witnessing his father being insulted by authorities, and in some instances, being beaten, left a bitter memory for Saber. However, just as Saber witnessed the growth of his father's business, he also observed the development of his own skills in managing challenges and risks along the journey. When I asked him what skills he is talking about, he mentioned learning Pashto language as an example, a skill that proved to be beneficial in many places en route:

Learning Pashto in our profession is vital because, ultimately, we have to pass through Pashtun territories. If we speak with them in their own language, they treat us much better, and if the person is not hostile, even a sense of friendship may develop between you.

A Rahbalad

When I asked Saber about the first time he independently undertook a journey, he referred to his first trip without his father's presence. It was a time when his father had gone to Quetta earlier, and a sensitive political issue happened in Kabul that necessitated sending an urgent letter to *Hizb-e Wahdat*'s office in Quetta. Since no one else was available, one of the *Hizb*'s officials asked him to accept this responsibility. Under the guise of a family trip, he, accompanied by two men, two women, and five children, accepted the responsibility of delivering the letter to Quetta. He performed this task and repeated such journeys to Quetta and later to Iran several times.

Travelling during that period was not like today. Since border control and passport systems were not as strict, convoys of vehicles could cross the long borders between Afghanistan, Pakistan, and Iran. Additionally, the open-door policies of both countries regarding Afghan refugees meant that these journeys, although lengthy, exhausting, and perilous, could yield results. Therefore, the term 'illegal' as used today did not have the same connotation for people regarding these movements. According to Saber, 'at that time, the land was God's land, and no one asked whether you had a passport or not. At the Pakistan border, when officials asked where you came from, we said Afghanistan, and they just recorded our names, took some money and had no further concerns.' If there were checkpoints and guards asked for bribes, it was the task of a *Rahbalad* to handle this and manage the entire arrangements from the start to the end of journey.

The years 1998 and 1999 were difficult times for Saber and his father. The Taliban had almost taken control of the whole country, persecuting religious and ethnic groups including Hazaras. Another phase of mass displacement began from Hazarajat. Hazaras were faced with discrimination, threats, and extrajudicial killings throughout the country. In this context, the elders in Yakawlang district in Bamiyan, where Saber was living, formed a *Shura* (local council) to discuss their options. In this council, a decision was made to send the young men and teenage boys to Iran as they were most exposed to danger should they remain in Afghanistan. Saber recalls from the council that after much discussion about the future and possibilities, 'almost everyone agreed that dark days awaited the people, and the best course of action was to send the youth and family members to Iran or Pakistan'.

After the decision was made, the discussion turned to how to send them. The debate began about which route to take and with whose assistance. Two elders requested his father's opinion and asked him to accept this responsibility to act as a guide, leading the people to safety. His father accepted, and it was decided that he would make a journey to Herat to coordinate the journey arrangements with his fellow *Rahbalad* there, and two months later, they would set out. However, on the way back from Herat to Bamiyan, he was arrested and detained by the

Taliban militia. Faced with this unforeseen problem, the council sought a new solution and, after much deliberation, realised they had no option but to turn to Saber to assume his father's role. Saber explains:

> I had to assume the responsibility and take our villagers to Iran. My father had already done all the coordination; all I had to do was to take the people to Herat and from there to the border with the help of my father's colleagues.

The decision to migrate, especially under such perilous conditions, was not taken lightly by the community. It involved extensive discussions and consensus-building within the *Shura*, reflecting a deeply ingrained practice among the Hazaras. The *Shura* played a critical role in decision-making on social matters during crisis periods. This collective approach ensured that decisions were made in the best interest of the community, considering all potential risks and benefits. This sense of duty among Hazara community leaders was extended to ensuring that those who migrate are in the hands of trusted and capable *Rahbalads* who are not just guides but also protectors and leaders.

Taking on the responsibility that his father had left behind was not an easy task for Saber. The journey from Bamiyan to Herat and then across the border into Iran required meticulous planning and coordination. The first step was gathering the group of villagers who had decided to make the perilous journey. This involved meetings and careful discussions with each family to ensure that everyone understood the risks and responsibilities involved. The journey from Bamiyan to Herat took three days. He had to arrange one pickup and a minibus to take the group to

Herat. To minimise the risks, they put the boys among the families in the minibus to make sure they were not very visible. Saber also had to pay bribes at every checkpoint along the route. After reaching the limits of vehicular access, the group continued the rest of their journey on foot, traversing mountains and villages. However, what most proved invaluable was his ability to negotiate with local elders and checkpoints guards in Pashto:

> I tried to be friendly as much as possible and speak to them in Pashto. Pashtuns and Talibs are very proud of their language, and when someone speaks to them in their language, they become very happy… To avoid trouble and conflict, you should try to show yourself as a friend of the Pashtun people. Besides that, for instance, if you address any of the soldiers as 'Mullah Sahib' they will be pleased and it will at least prevent them from starting a conflict with you from the beginning.

Upon reaching Herat, Saber met with his father's colleague, who was an experienced *Rahbalad* himself. He provided crucial support and advice, helping Saber to reconsider the route and ensure the safety of the group. They discussed the best routes to take, the checkpoints to avoid, and the bribes that might be necessary to smooth their passage. The network of *Rahbalad* was extensive and helped Saber to build strong relationships with many people along the route.

The next phase of the journey involved crossing into Iran via Pakistan, a task that required the assistance of two other *Rahbalads* at the border, one Hazara and one Baluch. The detour was critical due to the high presence of Taliban patrols along the Afghanistan-Iran border and the fear of militia groups and criminal gangs which made a direct crossing too dangerous. The Hazara *Rahbalad*, who was well-known in the community for his reliability and connections, helped to arrange safe passage through the most dangerous parts of the route. He coordinated with the Baloch *Rahbalad*, who had extensive knowledge of the border areas and could navigate the group through the difficult terrain. The Baloch *Rahbalad*'s role was particularly crucial when it came to crossing the actual border to Pakistan and from there to Iran. He guided them through the barren deserts and rugged mountains, often using little-known paths to avoid detection by militia. The journey was exhausting, and the group had to move quickly, with little rest, to minimise the risk of being caught. They had to ensure that everyone stayed together, especially the children and elderly, who were more vulnerable:

> If someone got lost on those routes then their fate was in God's hand as we didn't have the time to stop and search for the lost otherwise more people's lives would be at risk.

Upon crossing into Iran, the group still had a long way to go to reach Tehran.

They had to navigate through different cities, avoiding border patrols and police. Saber and the Hazara Rahbalad took charge during this phase, using their connections to find safe houses and arrange transport. The journey from the border to Taftan through Pakistan territory and farther to Zahidan was all on foot, a test of endurance and willpower. The group faced hunger, thirst, and the constant threat of capture:

Figure 2.1 The route that Saber took to take the group to Iran

Our journey was in the summer, so the weather was very hot, especially in Taftan and Zahedan. Many people suffered from heatstroke. There was a shortage of water. The wells along the way had water, but drinking it made us sick. Almost all the children got diarrhoea and became ill.

However, after ten days and frequent stops along the way, they reached Qom and then Tehran:

We delivered most of the group to their families and relatives in Isfahan, Qom, Tehran, and later in Mashhad. When we reached, for example, Qom, we would go to one of the relatives' houses, and everyone would get off there. Then we would inform people from our village in that city that the group had arrived in Qom and was at a certain person's house. After that, people would come to see if their parents, siblings, or close relatives were in the group or not. If they were, they would take them to

their own homes... Each time someone was taken, it felt
like a burden was lifted off my shoulders.

Saber's successful navigation of this journey and his ability
to safely lead his group to Iran earned him significant respect
and recognition within the community. This was no small feat,
as becoming a recognized *Rahbalad* required not only skill and
bravery but also a strong network and an impeccable reputation. Trust was paramount, and Saber had proven himself to be
trustworthy.

The ethnic network played a crucial role in this recognition. These
networks extended across borders, connecting communities in
Afghanistan, Pakistan, and Iran. The interconnectedness provided a support system for those on the move, offering places
of refuge, assistance, and information along the way. Saber lever-
aged these networks to facilitate the journey. In each major stop
along the route, there were trusted individuals and families who
provided shelter and support. These connections were not just
practical but also emotional, offering a sense of continuity and
community even in the most challenging circumstances. The
strong ties within this network also meant that news of Saber's
successful journey spread quickly. Word-of-mouth recommen-
dations were powerful, and soon more people sought Saber's
assistance for their journeys. His reputation as a reliable and honourable *Rahbalad* grew, further embedding him within the network of trusted guides.

In addition to the support from ethnic networks, Saber also ben-
efited from his father's reputation. Among the Hazaras, relationships and reputations were built over generations, and Saber's

family had a long history of serving the community. His father's legacy as a respected *Rahbalad* provided a strong foundation for Saber to build upon, and his successful journey further solidified his standing. Of course, his own qualities contributed to his recognition too. His ability to speak Pashto, his knowledge of the routes, and his skill in negotiating with various actors along the routes were all critical. His calm demeanour and decisive actions under pressure, which I personally witnessed on my journey with him, reassured those he guided, fostering a deep sense of trust.

A Qachaqbar

After the fall of the Taliban in 2001, Saber moved to Herat and settled there with his family. His father opened a small grocery shop and, beside that, started to work as a *Hawaladar* as a side job. In a country where formal banking systems were either unreliable or inaccessible to most, *Hawala* networks provided a crucial service, enabling the transfer of money over long distances and across borders. Saber's father's connections and trust within these networks were invaluable, establishing a foundation for their economic activities.

Saber, alongside helping his father, ventured into the food business by opening a small restaurant in a Hazara neighbourhood in Herat. His customers were predominantly Afghans travelling to and from the Iranian border. Many were returnees or those seeking a better life in Iran. The difficulty and expense of obtaining visas made regular migration channels prohibitive, pushing many towards irregular means. Saber, busy with restaurant work, put his work as a *Rahbalad* aside and travelled only once a year to visit relatives and friends. He remembers that 'people were coming to me to cross the border, but the [restaurant] business was good and I didn't have any time, so I referred them to others.'

The years 2005–2006 marked a significant change in the dynamics of border crossings between Afghanistan and Iran. Increased border security and the construction of walls on parts of the Iranian side of the border made traditional routes more perilous and less feasible for smugglers. Consequently, the smuggling networks shifted their operations towards the southwest, using Pakistan as a transit route. Zaranj, the capital of Nimruz province, emerged as a crucial hub for these networks due to its strategic location and the porous nature of its border.

By 2010, Saber faced increasing difficulties in Herat. Corruption was rampant, and local authorities, along with criminal gangs, frequently extorted money from business owners. The extortion became so burdensome that Saber found himself with little to no profit after paying off these demands:

> Life had become very tough in Herat... Not only me but any trader or anyone whose situation seemed a bit better was targeted by them… In the last few years, I paid them so much in bribes and extortion monthly that there was nothing left for myself at the end of the month. For people like me who had nobody to back them, there was no future in Herat.

He decided to move to Zaranj, a city he knew well and where he had established connections. A friend suggested a partnership in purchasing a hotel, seeing the potential for profit in catering to the needs of migrants and smugglers. Saber consulted with his father and agreed to the venture. They bought a hotel, which quickly became a bustling centre of activity, serving as a resting place and a meeting point for migrants and smugglers alike.

Describing Zaranj, Saber painted a vivid picture of a city thriving on smuggling, 'a city that has covered its face in dust like an unfortunate construction worker. But beneath this dust, it's all money and wealth,' he said. The city's economy is intricately linked to the smuggling of a variety of goods—motorbikes, fuel, drugs, household items, carpets, and medicine. However, migrant smuggling was among the most profitable trade, with Zaranj serving as the gateway for Afghans seeking to enter Iran irregularly. According to Saber, the city's survival depended on smuggling: 'everyone from any class or any business somehow passes their days with smuggling.' When I visited Zaranj in 2018, I understood what Saber meant. The local economy is intertwined with this illicit trade—drivers transport migrants, shopkeepers sell goods to them, hotel owners rent rooms, and restaurants provide food. Even the police and government officials are complicit, taking bribes from smugglers and migrants. As Saber explained: 'If they remove smuggling from Zaranj, nothing will be left but ruins and an empty plain.'

When I asked him about the legality of smuggling and people's perceptions of smugglers in Zaranj, Saber laughed and said:

> This is Afghanistan, which law? The law of the Afghan government that is corrupt from top to bottom? Or the law of the Iranian government that only knows oppression against Afghans?

He questioned the legitimacy of a government that failed to provide security or work for its people, arguing that such a government had no right to impose laws or define rights and duties. As he put it:

> People determine what is right and what is wrong. They say Haji Rahman [Saber's father] is a good person and Karzai is a corrupted one and the government says Karzai is good, Haji Rahman is bad. On the Judgment Day, who do you think God will prefer: Karzai or my father?

Saber's rhetorical question underscored the deep mistrust in formal state institutions and the alternative moral system that had emerged in their place. When I asked if he considered himself a *Qachaqbar*, Saber's response was both practical and philosophical: 'Well, some people call me *Rahbalad*, some call me a merchant, and others call me a *Qachaqbar*. Whatever name they call me, they still need me.'

Saber's role was far from easy. Managing a hotel in Zaranj is a complex and risky endeavour, involving constant interaction with migrants, smugglers, police, government officials, and other players. 'You just see the hotel, but it's a city in total chaos,' he said, highlighting the daily challenges and responsibilities he faced. He believes that trust and a good name is the key for a successful business in Zaranj and this trust was not lightly given:

> If I were a bad person, they wouldn't trust me to take their *namoos* [wives and daughters] and children through mountains and deserts. See, they trust me as someone who stands by his word and doesn't betray their honour. This is not a small talk. If the government says our job is illegal, who cares about the government? Who listens to this government?

Despite the challenges, Saber continues his work. The last time I spoke with him was in May 2024 via a WhatsApp call. I asked him how he was doing, and he said that his hotel was busy, and the number of Afghans travelling through Zaranj had increased since the return of the Taliban to power. When I asked him about the changes in the last three years, he replied with his usual humour: *'Khar haman khar ast, faghat palanesh avaz shodeh'* (the ass is the same old one, just its saddle has changed). He was trying to convey that it doesn't matter who is in power, whether it is Ashraf Ghani or the Taliban, the miseries and hardships of Afghanistan remain. As long as these difficulties persist, Afghans will be forced to migrate. My final question to him during our WhatsApp call was whether he had any plans to migrate himself. He responded:

> Migration requires courage and youth. I'm past that stage. I'm getting old and there is nothing for me in *Ghorbat* (exile). I've built a lifetime of reputation and respect here. Why would I go where no one knows me and I am no one?

I believe this statement encapsulates the depth of his connection as a *Qachaqbar* to his people and the complex realities of Afghan migration. It also reflects a broader theme in the Afghan migration: the struggle to maintain dignity and survive in the face of hardship and adversity, highlighting the deeply embedded realities of smuggling in Afghanistan, where personal and communal identities are intricately tied to the land and its enduring challenges.

Embedded realities: Some observations on the smuggling of migrants in Afghanistan

Through conversations with Saber and other Afghan smugglers, it became clear that the realities of Afghan migration are far more complex than official narratives typically convey. Afghan smuggling networks operate within a web of social, economic, and cultural factors that both drives and sustains them, revealing a picture that diverges from stereotypical portrayals of smugglers as mere exploiters of vulnerable populations. Instead, they are often seen as essential actors within their communities, providing services that, in the absence of state support, are necessary for survival and dignity. While rooted in the Afghan context, these insights resonate with migration dynamics in other regions facing similar challenges (Majidi, 2018). For ethnic communities like the Hazaras, smuggling networks have become embedded within their social and economic structures that offer resilience in the face of external pressures. Smugglers like Saber are not isolated criminals but integral members of their communities who uphold values and provide a measure of stability where the state structures fall short. This section offers a closer look at some of these insights, reflecting on broader implications for understanding irregular migration from Afghanistan.

Perceptions of the smuggling of migrants in Afghan communities

In Afghanistan, smuggling operates within a unique cultural framework where figures like smugglers have been often regarded as guides rather than criminals. Unlike the stereotypical image of a smuggler as a predatory actor exploiting the vulnerable, Afghan smugglers—especially among marginalised groups like the Hazaras—are seen as community figures who provide essential support in times of need. Historically, *Rahbalads* were responsible for guiding and protecting traders, pilgrims, and families through difficult terrain, offering not only navigation but also protection from external threats. While the modus operandi of these networks has evolved over the past two decades—such as the shift from the term *Rahbalad* (guide) to *Qachaqbar* (smuggler)—their role in the eyes of the community remains largely unchanged, as they continue to be perceived as guides who offer pathways to safety and opportunity in a landscape rife with danger and instability.

Saber's journey reflects this deeply rooted perception. Despite the hardships of his work, people continue to turn to him for help, trusting him to transport their families across borders. In his community, Saber embodies qualities that Afghan society holds in high regard: loyalty, resourcefulness, and a sense of moral duty to those he assists. This perception stands in stark contrast to international and state narratives, where smugglers are portrayed as grasping opportunists. For Afghan communities, however, Saber and others like him are regarded as more than mere facilitators—they are seen as figures who through their work uphold important values of honour and trust, despite the personal risks involved.

This alternative cultural framework challenges the dominant narrative that smuggling is solely an act of exploitation. In the Afghan context, smugglers are not just facilitators of migration but custodians of cultural and communal values, helping to maintain family unity, dignity, and survival. Within the Hazara community, smugglers have also played a crucial role in preserving kinship ties across borders. For families who face persecution and limited access to formal migration pathways, smugglers have been not merely service providers but are respected as key figures upholding the community's dignity and resilience. By connecting people with kin, protecting the vulnerable, and navigating uncertain terrain, smugglers like Saber are embedded in a cultural tradition that values survival, honour, and mutual support.

Economic dependence on smuggling

The economic impact of smuggling in certain Afghan regions, particularly border towns like Zaranj, is profound. In these areas, the local economy depends heavily on the steady flow of migrants and the associated demand for goods and services. In Zaranj, for instance, smuggling is a critical driver of local livelihoods, providing income for many individuals, from drivers and shopkeepers to hotel owners and food vendors. Smuggling sustains the community and has become woven into the region's economic fabric, allowing families to earn a living in ways they might otherwise be unable to achieve in a region with limited formal employment opportunities.

During my time in Zaranj, it became evident how deeply smuggling influences everyday life. The city's economy is shaped by a demand for services that cater to migrants: transportation, lodging, food, and even informal money transfer services are all tailored to facilitate the migration process. For people like Saber, running a hotel and connecting migrants with trusted routes offers a steady income that not only supports his family but also sustains the local economy. Businesses in Zaranj rely on the smuggling trade to such an extent that any disruption to this activity would likely destabilise the community and create significant hardship for those who depend on this economy.

Furthermore, international anti-smuggling policies, which seek to curb migration flows, rarely take into account these economic dependencies (MMC, 2021). Measures that target smuggling without addressing the economic realities risk causing more harm than good, leading to deeper poverty and insecurity. With few alternative economic prospects, local populations may be driven to adopt even riskier survival strategies, intensifying the need for migration rather than curbing it. This dependency has a ripple effect on the community, where smuggling acts as an economic stabiliser, ensuring that local residents can access income in a region largely overlooked by state economic planning. For Saber and his community, smuggling is not a criminal enterprise; it is an economic lifeline that sustains entire families, if not neighbourhoods, and provides stability amid an unpredictable economic landscape.

Community versus state narratives

The contrast between community and state narratives on smuggling reveals fundamental differences in how legitimacy and morality are defined. Official narratives frequently depict smuggling as an inherently criminal act associated with exploitation, framing smugglers as individuals who prey on vulnerable migrants, stripping them of agency and security. However, within

Afghan communities, particularly among those who directly benefit from smugglers' services, these figures are viewed in a far more positive light. Smugglers like Saber are seen as honourable and trustworthy individuals who fulfil a role that governments fail to provide, enabling safe passage, family reunification, and access to opportunities that would otherwise be out of reach.

In Afghan society, legitimacy is rooted less in state-imposed laws and more in the values of trust and reliability within the community. This is especially true in rural and marginalised communities where the state is perceived as an external force. Saber's story exemplifies this divergence in perception: while authorities might label his work as illegal, his community sees him as a necessary actor providing a vital service for survival. His community's trust is based not on his adherence to the law but on his reputation as a *Rahbalad* rather than a *Qachaqbar*—a guide who upholds promises, ensures safety, and facilitates paths to better futures. This community-based legitimacy not only challenges the state's criminalization of smuggling but also reflects broader tensions between community autonomy and state authority (Nimkar and Mohammadi, 2023). For Afghan communities, as long as the state fails to offer viable migration pathways, smuggling will continue to be seen as a morally acceptable, even essential, survival mechanism that aligns with communal values and shared goals.

The impact of state corruption on smuggling and perceptions

Corruption within Afghan state institutions significantly affects both the operations of smugglers and community perceptions of their legitimacy. Along Afghan migration routes, bribery is rampant, with smugglers frequently paying off officials to secure safe passage. This systemic corruption not only allows smuggling operations to thrive but also erodes public trust in the government. For smugglers like Saber, repeated demands for bribes at every checkpoint reinforce the view that the state acts less as a protective authority for Afghan citizens and more as a barrier that must be bypassed. Consequently, smugglers see themselves as essential service providers stepping into roles that the state should, ideally, fulfil. This environment of corruption serves as both a challenge and a justification for smugglers. The constant bribery demands create an added 'cost of doing business,' which Saber and others pay in exchange for performing critical roles that protect vulnerable people. This perspective distances smugglers from state-defined criminality, framing their work not as exploitative but as a necessary response to the state's failure to offer safe migration paths. To smugglers, the corruption they navigate legitimises their role, as they continue providing services that are otherwise unavailable through formal channels.

Corruption also shapes public perceptions of smuggling, reinforcing the community's view of smugglers as legitimate actors in a system plagued by state complicity and inefficiency. When communities witness police and officials accepting bribes, they perceive the state as ineffective and untrustworthy. For many, the state's inability to enforce fair practices or provide secure migration pathways severely undermines its authority, leaving communities with few choices but to rely on smugglers. This strengthens the view of smugglers as alternative providers of essential services, such as safe passage, guidance, and economic opportunity. Saber's rhetorical question about which authority—the state or the community—has the moral high ground echoes this sentiment. To him, as to many others, smugglers who honour their promises and uphold community values hold a legitimacy greater than that of a state compromised by corruption.

Moral frameworks and trust networks in Afghan smuggling

In Afghanistan, the perceived legitimacy of smuggling is largely shaped by moral frameworks deeply rooted in community values, kinship, and trust. While formal State perspectives often reduce smuggling to a legal issue, Afghan communities assess it based on its outcomes. If a smuggler like Saber successfully helps someone escape persecution, reunites a family, or provides a means of economic survival, his actions are viewed as morally justified, regardless of their legal standing. This moral legitimacy is intertwined with the concepts of trust and honour—values that are central to Afghan society and earned through consistent, reliable service. Trust is especially important in these networks, as smugglers who fulfil their promises and protect their clients' well-being build a reputation that becomes their most valuable asset (see: Nimkar and Mohammadi, 2023).

Saber's story illustrates how such trust is developed over years of service, through strong connections and a reputation for safeguarding clients' dignity. His ability to communicate in Pashto and navigate different cultural and political landscapes enhances his credibility, fostering relationships across ethnic divides that might otherwise be inaccessible. In Afghan communities, trust in a smuggler is often stronger than trust in the state, particularly among the Hazaras, where longstanding ethnic networks support migration both as a survival strategy and as a means to preserve dignity in the face of state neglect. For many, smugglers like Saber become respected figures who uphold the community's honour and protect values that formal systems fail to safeguard. This socially embedded trust framework, which holds smugglers to high standards of conduct, positions smuggling as a morally legitimate endeavour, embedded within Afghan society's resilience and adaptability.

Dependency on smugglers for survival and mobility

Contrary to assumptions that smugglers play a primary role in encouraging migration, Afghan smugglers more often serve as facilitators of already-made decisions. For families in crisis, the choice to migrate is not taken lightly and often follows lengthy discussions involving family members and community elders. For those facing persecution, economic hardship, or the desire to reunite with family members abroad, migration is a strategy for survival—sometimes a forced response to immediate threats and other times a spontaneous decision when unexpected opportunities arise. In this context, smugglers act as facilitators who provide the knowledge, resources, and logistical support necessary for a safe journey.

Once the decision to migrate has been made, reliance on smugglers like Saber becomes indispensable. Saber's extensive experience and knowledge of routes, border procedures, and local customs make him a valuable ally for migrants navigating perilous journeys. This dependency reflects the lack of formal support systems in Afghanistan, where the state's absence pushes migrants toward informal networks. The necessity of relying on smugglers for safety, food, and shelter makes their role critical in the migration journey, as smugglers offer both guidance and a degree of security.

Saber's role demonstrates that smugglers often do more than provide a route; they become temporary protectors, guiding families through unfamiliar terrain and offering assurance. The dependency on smugglers is therefore not solely a matter of logistics but a deliberate choice, rooted in the recognition of their role as guardians of survival in an unpredictable environment. For many Afghan migrants, smugglers represent not a vulnerability but a partnership—a way to navigate complex, high-risk journeys with a level of dignity and security that they would not otherwise possess.

3
Living on the doorstep: The Golshahr Ghetto

Atefeh Kazemi

Beyond the familiar alleys of Golshahr

Mashhad is a major city in Iran, especially renowned as a place of pilgrimage, attracting millions of religious tourists. On its outskirts, the Golshahr district may seem incongruent, like an awkward patch in the cultural fabric of the city. Although the northeast periphery of Mashhad is generally known as a disadvantaged area, Golshahr is tainted with additional layers of notoriety and stigma. Accommodating more than 40,000 Afghan migrants mostly of the Hazara ethnicity, it is recognized as an overcrowded neighbourhood of *Afghanis,* a term that has become one of abuse among Iranians.

The emergence of cafes and traditional Afghan restaurants in Golshahr, adorned with pictures of Hazarajat's natural beauty and historical landscapes, fails to tempt Iranian outsiders. The juxtaposition of the Afghanistan flag alongside Iran's flag standing on café counters finds its audience among no one but Hazara youth, most of whom, like me, have never lived in Afghanistan. However, in spite of the hostile, negative stereotypes circulating about Golshahr, I have often heard my Hazara peers refer to it as a haven—the safest place in Iran. For a Hazara boy after an exhausting day of digging wells or construction work, Golshahr would become a sanctuary, a place to momentarily escape the uncertainties that loom over our lives. In a music track named after the neighbourhood, Ali Amir, a Hazara rapper, describes Golshahr's atmosphere as different, as special—'it acts on us like a painkiller' (Amir 2019). The Golshahr alleys are, after all, inoffensive—nobody calls us *Afghani* there.

The intangible sense of safety in Golshahr was only revealed when abruptly stripped away as I left for Tehran in pursuit of a university education in 2015. Having successfully passed the

Figure 3.1 A café in Golshahr 2021—photo taken by Atefeh Kazemi

matriculation exam, the *Konkur*, I was accepted into the field of cinematography and was finally able to follow my passion. In high school, despite my interest in the arts, I studied Experimental Science, as Afghan nationals were restricted to theoretical fields (Mathematical, Experimental, and Human Sciences). Afghan students were also restricted in terms of what they could study at university and in which regions they could study. I felt lucky that I would be finally allowed to study what I wanted in university. We, Hazara youth, encountered so many obstacles in Golshahr, but we did not think of them as insurmountable barriers. Instead, when we faced a blockage in our way, we considered every possible option to finally find a way around it. The fact that everyone with a school diploma was allowed to sit the Konkur for art seemed to offer a chink in the barrier for me.

In our family, there was already a writer and a painter (my older sisters). Despite financial hardship, in Golshahr, a tendency towards literature and art prevails among Hazara youth. Specifically, poetry and writing circles have always been popular, although many parents (typically first-generation) are illiterate. Regardless of the duration of residence, level of education or any other factors, all Afghan migrants are restricted to labour-intensive work, such as construction for men, which does not pay enough to support their families. Mothers in many families contribute to the household costs by working on farmlands, in *korki* (wool-cleaning workshops), or doing piece work, pistachio cracking, or beading at home. Many students, like myself, had to work in sewing workshops during the summer holidays to save up money for their school education fees. For me, literature and art were the only ways to be able to imagine and think beyond the restricted scale of life in the community. The idea of studying cinematography was a dream come true. However, soon after I moved to Tehran, my excited dream smashed into the concrete walls of those boundaries.

On my first day in Tehran, Sooreh University, to which I had secured entry, refused to register me. One of the administrative staff, Mr. Shafiqi who was a middle-aged man in charge of new entry registration, flatly stated: 'You are Afghani'. When I insisted, he lost his temper, almost shouting: 'I corresponded with *Sazman-e Sanjesh* (Examinations Board) many times last year to not send Afghani students to this academy'. The fact that after many years, I can still clearly remember what he said is sad. I remained entirely silent, as uttering even one word would risk me bursting into tears. Then he explained that the ambiguous residence document of Afghan students was the reason, even though the true reason was already explicitly expressed. Although the denial of my entry into that art academy was arbitrary, my several appeals to the Foreign Educational Affairs Organization were of no help.

Nonetheless, having prepared for the *Konkur* (university admission) exam for months to quit seemed ridiculous to me. I was accustomed to negotiating the barriers to my education. The Education Minister of Iran issued new directives every year regarding the registration of Afghan nationals in schools, and we had to wait to see what problems they would bring and how we could get around them. Concerns about the prospective rise in fees or additional restrictions always cast a shadow over the summer holidays. Typically, the directive usually arrived just a few days ahead of the start of term, with very limited capacity left for new entries to the schools. However, at least in Golshahr, we were not alone in our dreads and hopes. This time, as the only Afghan in an all-Iranian cohort, I felt like an outcast with problems peculiar to me.

For me, insisting on my right to study this course was the only way. I waited for Mr. Shafiqi and other staff in the corridor of the university's administrative section for several mornings in a row. Most of the time, after repeating my demand, I was silenced by the condescending monologues of Mr. Shafiqi, which oscillated awkwardly between rationalising his refusal and contemptuous pity. Finally, my efforts paid off. The university allowed me to pay my tuition and attend classes on the condition that I obtain a student visa. While proceeding with the registration, Mr. Shafiqi asked me 'Why do you want to study cinematography? It is something masculine and even if we accept your entry you will not succeed as you are a woman.' 'I am sure I can,' I responded with conviction. He then promised that he would make this process so hard for me that I would myself bring him my withdrawal letter to sign, like the other Afghani student last year. When I was going through the process of changing my residence permit into a student visa, I realised what he meant. The process needed signatures from the administrative staff multiple times, and Mr. Shafiqi was the one who always managed to get away with not doing it. Moreover, tuition was expensive for me and I needed to work more part-time hours, adding to the difficulties.

I was staying at my sister's home in a distant southern suburb of Tehran, commuting two hours early every morning to the University in dilapidated minibuses with day labourers. Attending classes, in which my name was yet to be listed, with carefree Iranian peers coming mainly from the middle class, had sharpened the contrast of my peculiarity. Moreover, my typical Hazara phenotype, marking me out as *Afghani*, exposed me to questions about my origins each time I met someone new. In all cases, I insisted 'I am from Mashhad', an unsatisfying answer. In Tehran, I hid my identity not only to avoid a more explicit exclusion but also because, emerging from the cocoon of Golshahr, my self-image had been shattered into many pieces, making it difficult sometimes to configure who I am. I tried hard to speak Farsi with a Tehrani accent and to reshape my eyes with make-up.

I was a determined woman but, maybe, not strong enough to resist the racism I faced. Consequently, on one of the rainy days of that autumn, I finally withdrew my still incomplete registration, as Mr. Shafiqi had foreseen. A few days before, I had cut my long hair as short as I could and stopped wearing make-up. It was not driven by a conscious sense of feminism but by pure frustration. Later I started pursuing my education in anthropology at another university in Tehran. Although deflected from my initial ambitions, this experience of exclusion sparked new aspirations and a new trajectory.

The complicated procedures of becoming a university student for our generation of Iran-born Hazaras was a difficult rite of passage, marking entry into a new realm of potential interaction with Iranian mainstream society but in a capacity other than labourers, which is how we are typically seen. This procedure involved a bureaucratic process to change our annual residence permit as a *muhajir* (migrant) to a student visa. It takes nearly six months and concludes with travelling to Afghanistan to apply for an Iranian visa and entering Iran as a foreign student. This journey was deemed risky, though, particularly for girls crossing the Afghanistan borders by land. It was a significant concern and a reason for families to discourage their daughters from pursuing university education, especially because most of us could not afford a flight, which was safer. Another worry for the families was the risk of the student's residence permit not being extended after graduation. For some families, it meant casting more uncertainty over our future, as having higher education would not broaden our job opportunities beyond the permitted menial occupations.

In the Mashhad passport office, by chance, I met one of my Golshari high school classmates, Fatemeh, who, like me, was alone on this journey. We planned to go together to Herat as it was much more convenient in terms of distance and expenses than Kabul, the capital. We hired a taxi driver for a round trip to Herat, which was four hours away from Mashhad. The border checkpoint was crammed with people returning to Afghanistan with their possessions packed in large cheap bags. After several hours of waiting there, we crossed the border and could continue our journey to Herat. Along the way, at Dogharon, we stopped at a UNHCR camp. We were given a Voluntary Repatriation Form to complete, and we each received a grey blanket with a UNHCR label on it, a pack of biscuits, and a bar of soap. Then we were directed to the Ansar Camp, established for returnees from Iran and located in a remote suburb of the city. When we arrived it was evening. The camp operator was reluctant to accommodate us, claiming it was not safe enough and he did not want to shoulder the responsibility for two young women. He finally let us in when he saw we literally had nowhere else to stay and it was getting dark.

I experienced Herat neither through the eyes of an Iranian visitor nor a person visiting their motherland. My identity lacked the authenticity for either perspective. Both my parents were children when they arrived in Iran with their families. Consequently, we had no property or social ties left in Afghanistan to make me feel less of a stranger to the soil I am officially identified with. Yet, there was a vague sense of familiarity, reminiscent of my feelings of alienation in Iran, especially when local people in Herat referred to us as *zavarak*. This sense of familiarity grew even more tangible when two boys riding on a motorcycle hit us with rotten oranges, calling us *Iranigak*, when we were on our way back to camp. *Zavarak* in Afghanistan's Farsi means 'little passenger' and *Iranigak* means 'little Iranian' both with ridiculing connotations. The terms *zavarak* and *Iranigak* had a strong shared significance with *Afghani*, which we are called in Iran, carrying the same harsh message 'You do not belong here.' In Herat women typically wore burqas which we were not used to. Instead, our chadors, combined with our distinctive Iranian accent, made us stand out from local Herati women.

After a week in Herat, when I was back in Iran, I found very little to share about my experience in Afghanistan. Our journey did not involve visits to tourist sites or sightseeing. Instead, it was just a challenging part of a bureaucratic ritual we accomplished and swiftly returned. On my way back home, on the bus to Golshahr, an old Hazara woman called me *allay* (meaning dear in the Hazara dialect), asking me to pass her bus card to the driver.

When I looked at her wrinkled and smiling face, I felt a familiar sense of connection once again.

Golshahr, a place of conflicting feelings

When I was back in Golshahr the sense of safety that it gave me was delicious—it felt like frost-nipped skin enjoying a pleasant tingling from the heat of the fire. However, it was an incomplete pleasure, something was missing that was not clear to me and which I still think about. My experience in Tehran and Herat opened my eyes to the incongruity of my situation as a *muhajir* and left me confused. I started to talk about this to other people and my peers in Golshahr. We were a generation of ambivalence—foreigners in our country of birth, migrants without having ever migrated, 'Iranian Afghans'. Meanwhile, Golshahr was the only space capable of holding all these paradoxes together. In Golshahr, we were neither *Afghani* nor *Iranigak*.

We had a more dignified term to introduce ourselves: *muhajir*. The first time that I realized the specific meaning of this term was during my first days in elementary school. The teacher was asking us our names alongside our fathers' jobs. It soon turned into a tedious chain of names with the recurring motif of 'worker' uttered by different voices. The Afghan students needed to mention their nationality as well, and I did so as *Afghani*. It was an elementary school in the neighbouring district, and although the number of Afghan students was significant, they were not the majority as in the schools in Golshahr. That day, one of my Afghan classmates took me aside and told me 'Don't say "I am an

Afghani" instead, say you are "muhajir".' At that moment of child-hood, I understood that this term, *Afghani*, was associated with something shameful.

The word *Afghani* is not inherently disdainful, though, and we often use it among ourselves. However, in the mouths of Iranians, this word turns into something contemptuous. The term *Afghani* is heavily inflected by the insults it is often accompanied by when used by Iranians until it has gradually become an independent insult itself. On the other hand, *muhajir* was an umbrella term in Iranian Farsi to describe migration of any kind. It has also been a term that the Iranian government often uses to refer to Afghans in Iran, carefully avoiding the term 'refugee', which entails poten-tial responsibilities. Nonetheless, not being loaded with racially humiliating connotations was the only privileged aspect of this term for me.

In Golshahr, we speak a blend of Hazaragi and Farsi with a Mashahdi accent, which is informally known as the *Golshahri* accent and considered by Iranians as slang. In school, we tried our best to speak Iranian Farsi to be polite. Although schools in Iran are places for homogenising and assimilating diverse ethnic identities into the central Fars culture, the process was somehow different for us. We were being trained to blend into the society from which we are excluded. This was the true meaning of '*muhajir*' for me: living on the margins. Ironically, the peripheral location of Golshahr resembles our situation in Iranian urban society. For our Iran-born generations, '*muhajir*' is also implicitly perceived as an agreeable word for a disagreeable concept: *Iranian-Afghan*. This is a hyphenated compound term that is never used. Not just because it is an arbitrary word in terms of Iran's constitutional law, but also because it seems to reveal something odd and incompatible. Iran's constitution confers Iranian nationality only to the child born to an Iranian father. Granting citizenship to children born to Iranian mothers and non-Iranian fathers has been a source of controversy for years and is still in dispute. So, the word 'Iranian-Afghan' sounds paradoxical.

What would a hyphen, located between two sharply divided realms of existence, two racially dichotomized identities, uncover? It would violate the rules of classification and upset the balance of the boundaries. Therefore, we *muhajir*s are hybrid creatures who speak a dissonant combination of accents, situated between the realms and, thus, lacking purity. I often feel this sense of alienation whenever we are referred to as *atba-e biganeh* (alien nationals) by the officials or in formal texts. These concerns about purity have a more visible reflection in health-care regulations, based on which, for example, organ transplantation or blood donation between Afghan *muhajir*s and Iranians is strictly banned. On social media, I happened to read of my peers' experiences of rejection at blood donation centres where their blood donation was neither welcomed nor accepted, causing many complex feelings in them.

However, I am not surprised that our parents or grandparents were not keen on passing down a sense of traditional ethnic identity to us. For them, it might have aroused a deep-seated fear on both sides of the border—excluded as Hazara in Afghanistan, and *Afghanis* in Iran. My mother once told me about expulsion schemes during the mid-1990s, under which the police officers were searching for *Afghanis* in the neighbourhood, door by door.

Terrified, she took us children and went to an Iranian neighbour's house to hide. She told me some parents even faced empty homes coming back from work to find their children arrested. As 'Hazaras', they were seriously at risk of being killed by Taliban forces in Afghanistan (see Chapter 1). Narrating these stories must have left a bitter taste in her mouth, which made it hard for her to speak further about our traditional identity.

However, Golshahr chooses not to dwell on the old stories of suffering. Golshahr is a place to move on and a place to forget. This sentiment is also reflected in the pulsating flow of the people across Shulugh Bazar (literally meaning crowded market). This open-air market is not significant simply for its commercial capacity where cheaper vegetables and fruits are always available. In addition, it is a pivotal social space for Golshahr residents, a place that connects individuals to a dense social network, where starting small talk with friends met by chance, relatives or even strangers is easy. It serves as a resource for staying informed about the ever-changing government directives and procedures for *muhajir*s as well as the current news and rumours in the districts. At the end of Shulugh Bazar, there's a space where old Hazara men gather, seemingly for peddling. However, whenever I saw them, they were busy talking to each other rather than actually selling and buying. Their items are limited to combs, radio wires, and chargers for old-fashioned cell phones like Nokia, alongside turquoise and agate stone rings. The main item, though, is their stories of the past and their memories. Like their wares, their narratives are becoming more and more obsolete, fading away in the hustle and bustle of Shulugh Bazar.

Figure 3.2 The Hazara elders at the end of the Shulugh Bazar 2020—photo taken by Atefeh Kazemi

Golshahr stories are not fixed by those harsh winters and the summer harvests in Hazarajat nor the burnt lands and long periods of war, often told by the elders, the first generation of migration. While encapsulating an imagined home within its bounds, Golshahr continues to unfold new stories of struggles for survival and resilience. It embodies the confusion and struggle of the young generation, still in search of their identity. Accommodating thousands of *muhajirs,* Golshahr has been infected by the stigma attached to its residents. Therefore, among most of the Hazara youth, not only is *Afghani* a contemptuous word, but *Golshahr* is also unmentionable, even while commuting from the city. Instead, Tollab (a neighbouring district) is often given as an address, especially by women and girls. Nonetheless, on some occasions, when giving the real address becomes unavoidable, the situation can turn ugly. My sister, Elaha, recalled the night that her university course finished late after the buses had stopped running. When she was trying to get a taxi, many of them refused to take her to Golshahr.

Many years and even borders away, former Golshahr residents still remember it with conflicting feelings. Ali Ahmadi Dovlat starts his book, 'Golshahr: Memories of a Geologist' with this sentence: 'I love Golshahr, the town of my yesterday's fears and hopes.' Reading his book, I was perplexed by this question 'What has he missed so much about Golshahr?' His memoir accurately reflects the uncertainty and restrictions of *muhajirs'* lives in Golshahr and weaves a sense of connection in the *muhajir* audience through the recounting of his own life. It reflects the complex sense of belonging to Golshahr where *muhajirs* had the opportunity to develop a sense of 'inclusion' within a collective experience of 'exclusion'. Thinking of my own experience in Golshahr, it was not a desirable place to live. My sisters and I hated Golshahr as it was located in a remote and notorious corner of the city. It was one of the reasons that I was enthusiastic about pursuing my education in another city, assuming that out of Golshahr I could be free from Golshahr's stigma. However, soon after I left Golshahr for Teheran, I realised that I would not be free from the stigma of being recognized as an *Afghani* in Iran. At least Golshahr had sheltered me from the sense of being singled out, as we were all *muhajirs*. Golshahr was a place of exclusion, yet a place of safety that I felt more vividly upon returning.

In Iranian society, the Hazara *muhajirs* would often be singled out. It is not solely based on the Hazaragi phenotype but also because of the restrictions posed by our residence permit. The majority of Afghan refugees, including Hazaras, live under the Amayesh scheme, which is renewed annually and grants holders permission to stay in a province and apply for work permits in given job categories during their validity period. Lacking an Iranian *cod-e melli* (national ID number) means deprivation of or limited access to many public services such as health insurance, education, or bank services since this code is required on most platforms. Even the process for accessing the available services is often different and usually cumbersome for us. This *ID code deficiency* sometimes felt like an unusual disability, particularly that semester in July 2018 when I was compelled to take my final exams in a segregated room for 'special cases'.

Several days before, I had been unable to print my exam card, and the registration staff, in response, explained that I was expected to show my extended resident permit to her to be able to take my exams. However, without informing me or giving any warning beforehand, she had already suspended my student portal and excluded me from the final exams. After an appeal to the university administration, I could only obtain permission to take my exams under the category of 'special cases', in a room set aside for disabled students. It was crowded and noisy as every student had a companion to help them with reading the questions or writing their answers. It felt deeply awkward when a member of staff inquired whether I had a companion, wondering what kind of disability I had.

Later on, when one of the members of an NGO that was working with Afghan *muhajir*s in Iran asked me to join them in their campaign, I was disappointed with the campaign's title. It was *tawanmand-sazi muhajirin-e Afghan* (meaning in literal translation enabling/empowering Afghan *muhajirs*). It reminded me of that awkward experience of July that year. This word *tawanmand-sazi* (to enable/empower) is often used by the associations who work with people with disabilities, addiction, or mental illness— people who presumably are unable to engage fully in society..

On the contrary, living among *muhajirs*, Golshahr was the place that gave, to some extent, the pleasure of feeling ordinary. It is a place where suffering takes on a specific character. When shared, not only does it become more bearable but also normalised. There is where the *muhajirs* are not alone in having problems with opening a bank account or owning a SIM card for their mobile phones and many other restrictions. Golshahr has even had its own pulp comedian groups, who often send up such challenges in their video clips. However, the dense social network among us in Golshahr has always functioned as more than just a source of empathy. It is through the warp and woof of Golshahr's social network that the Hazara youth continue to find their way through barriers imposed on them, although it is not necessarily the story of success.

Many self-governing institutions such as literature associations, charities, and schools have been developed by *muhajirs* to fulfil some of their unmet needs. One of these institutions is the *Afghani* schools. Although every year many *muhajir* students are excluded from registration in official schools, whether for the lack of capacity, documents, or financial problems, there are self-governing schools for them in Golshahr. While I have not personally attended these schools, a visit some years ago and a conversation with an administrator brought back memories from elementary school. I remember the schoolmaster called a list of names and then pushed those children out of the line and I no longer saw them in the school. The *Afghani* school is where two groups of excluded people coexist. *Muhajir* teachers, often unemployed university students or graduates, due to work permit limitations teach *muhajir* students who were expelled or unable to join official schools. The teachers often face financial struggles, with months passing without wages as the students are unable to pay their tuition on time.

Though some of us were compelled to study in the dilapidated buildings of these schools with low-quality copies of the official schoolbooks, out of Golshahr we practised the shared aspects of our identity with Iranians, trying to ignore these stigmatised experiences which differentiated us from them. During high

Figure 3.3 A self-governing school in Golashahr 2015—photo taken by Atefeh Kazemi

school, I attended writing workshops held at the Eshraq institution, located in the central part of the city. In those workshops, there was another girl, Zahra, who looked Hazara. However, her Iranian accent was very good. Both of us were hiding our identity as *muhajirs*. One day I saw her working in a stationery shop in Golshahr, and I was sure she was a *muhajir*. In the next writing workshop, I tried to hint that I too was *muhajir*, but she would not let down her guard. Leaving the workshop one day, I asked which way she was going. She said she lived on Tollab Boulevard. Even more confident I said, '*I live in Golshahr*'. That night on our way back home in the Golshahr bus we shared our experiences of hiding our identity, laughing all the way back, pleased to find a lot in common.

For some people of my generation, art and literature were not only a way to break free from the confines of *muhajirhood* but also a form of resistance. The Selma Theatre Group, active in Golshahr in recent years, embodies this spirit. This group was initiated and nurtured by the ideas of Alireza Saeedi, who has devoted a significant part of his life to teaching acting to *muhajir* youth for free. I have known him since his activities in Tehran in 2016. Alireza views theatre not just as an art form but also as therapy and a means of social change. To this end, discussion sessions are a pivotal part of their activities, and their performance themes are often interwoven with the experiences and narratives of the *muhajirs*. Over the past few years, he has sought to attract audiences from both Golshahr and other parts of the city, in an attempt to break the negative stereotypes against *Afghanis* and Golshahr.

For their first performance in Golshahr, they created a stage in an abandoned library named Resalat. However, they were compelled to leave after several months. Eventually, they managed to secure a dilapidated and desolate *Ab Anbar*, a large underground cistern, designed to store and cool drinking water. It took a few months for them to repair the building and turn it into a venue for their weekly public performances. The fact that most male members of the group were skilled in construction work significantly compensated for their lack of financial budget. The group functions as a network for cooperation, and their performances were often free. Currently, the group is displaced once again, as they had to move out of the *Ab Anbar* after about two years.

One may wonder, 'What are they in search of in such a remote margin of the city?'. During the days I spent with them, engaged in preparations for one of their performances titled *Adan* (Eden) focused on the narratives of refugee camps, I perceived their endeavour as a manifestation of resistance within the *muhajir's* life. Ironically, their own circumstances mirror the trajectory of a *muhajir*—constantly on the move, lacking a stable place to call their own. They have been displaced multiple times from the places where they have striven to adapt and belong. Despite the uncertainty of their circumstances, they are trying to develop, even if they are not sure how or where it will lead or if it will continue. They create social spaces from abandoned and forgotten places, turning them into areas where *muhajir* youth can share their voices with people from other generations and possibly outside their community.

Figure 3.4 'Spectator of Death' by Selma Theatre Group, photo taken by Mohammad Saeedi

Rooting and departure

Golshahr has changed significantly from how I remember it in my childhood—many Afghan traditional restaurants, Afghan clothes stores, and cafes have sprung up. These traditional restaurants are where I first in my life tasted many Afghan foods like *manto* and *ashak*. Some of my generation express a strong sense of belonging to Golshahr. However, it never felt genuinely like home to me. There is something about Golshahr that opposes the concept of home.

If a home is to be defined as a place where you have the right to stay and return, how can I call Golshahr home? We are constantly reminded that we are not welcome in Iran and that our stay is temporary. This temporariness is constantly underlined by the need to renew the temporary residence permit every year.

The annual residency permit under the *Amayesh* scheme was mostly for those who, like our family, had come to Iran in the early decade of the Islamic revolution and usually is out of reach for those Afghans who came later. However, even this temporary residence permit can be easily cancelled or revoked. The frequency and duration of trips outside Iran are strictly limited and controlled, and any violation leads to the cancellation of the residence permit. People under the *Amayesh* scheme would lose their residence permit if they left the country. For passport holders with more mobility options, leaving Iran for longer than the permitted period (three months for regular passports) has to be an irrevocable decision and a one-way journey. This politics of border control makes the price of mobility very heavy emotionally. Also, it reveals the vulnerability of our roots and ties to our country of birth and residence, while exposed to the rigid rules of the border. Under such circumstances, 'return' to Iran, to the place of our birth or childhood, is only possible for us as tourists who pay for a visa and are allowed to stay for a limited time.

As living in Iran gives us no prospect of inclusion, the idea of leaving is a seed planted in our minds from the early days and grows with us gradually. In the mid-2000s, an International Organization for Migration (IOM) programme for educated *muhajirs* opened a new, though vague, opportunity offering a dignified job and a reasonable wage for the *muhajir* youth (see next chapter). It also became a source of inspiration for many of us to pursue a university degree and move to our country of origin after graduation. Like many other *muhajir* graduates, my brother Ali applied for the IOM scheme, awaited their recruitment, and finally left for Afghanistan in 2010. A couple of years later, my sister Elaha followed the same route. However, the hope for the future was accompanied by concerns about safety among the Hazara families. Since Elaha's and Hassan's departure, my mother had been anxiously following any news about Kabul, especially West Kabul, Dasht-e Barchi, where Elaha and Hassan resided. This district, inhabited mostly by the Hazaras, was occasionally targeted by suicide bombers.

Roots may be seen as attachments to the places you lived and the people with whom you lived and have a history. However, Golshahr is not a place to put down roots, as departure is always looming. We are called *muhajirs* and deemed *displaced* upon our birth in Iran even though we have not migrated, and yet it seems, we inevitably assume and internalise this identity.

For some people, the price of departure would be weighed against the risk of death. Between 2012 and 2015, more and more people in Golshahr were preparing themselves for irregular migration towards the West. During that time, we frequently heard of families auctioning off all their household items of furniture to pay for their migration. I can remember that my mother and I bought a set of cooking utensils from someone who was leaving. The atmosphere was tense, and the young mother was visibly agitated, struggling to determine the prices, especially for items received as wedding gifts. We bought a pot set, which I never felt comfortable cooking in and rarely used.

Many people have left (and leave) Golshahr in different ways and in various directions. Several years later, many of them come back to Iran as international tourists from various countries to visit their families and relatives, often helping them economically. But for some, like our neighbour, *Nane Aman* (Aman's mother), the waiting never ends. For more than a decade, she has waited for a word from her daughter and son, the passengers on a refugee boat to Australia. On sunny days, sitting in front of the mosque in the streets where sometimes other elder women join her helps her with the painfulness of waiting which is now a part of her life. The bustling streets of Golshahr might be somehow therapeutically distractive for her. The lively flow of people in Golshahr's streets never stops and Golshahr does not remember those who are lost. Golshahr, with those invisible walls surrounding it, is a place to move on from.

4

'Return' as new exile

Reza Hussaini

Forced and voluntary return

I tried to walk faster but not so fast that it would look like running, which would let the Iranian police know that I (as an Afghan-Hazara) was scared and trying to flee. I didn't look back, fearing they might notice. As soon as I got near the house, my hand froze on the doorbell, until the door opened and I jumped inside, relieved that I had once again evaded the *Afghani-Begir* (Afghan catching) police. It was the summer of 1995, and I was 16, living in Golshahr, Mashhad, Iran, as an Afghan forced migrant. I was always vigilant, my eyes constantly scanning the distance for police cars to avoid being caught off guard by the *Afghani-Begir* police. Even though I had a residency card (Blue card), it was of no use because if the police caught me, they would just tear it up and then issue a deportation letter to Afghanistan. Things were bad then for Afghan-Hazara in Iran; the arrest and forced deportation of Afghans was rampant, as it is nowadays (UNHCR 2024).

At that time, the forced return/deportation of Afghans was always portrayed as 'voluntary return' in the Iranian media. This was the case while Afghanistan was still at war, and the newly emerged Taliban were openly hostile towards the Hazaras (the largest migrant population residing in Iran), which later led to the mass killings of Hazaras in Mazar Sharif (1998) and Bamiyan (2001) (see Chapter 1). In discussions with family and friends about going/returning to Afghanistan, we never used the term 'voluntary return'. We used the word *Rad-e-Marz*, which literally means to forcibly expel someone across the border and get rid of him or her. *Rad-e-Marz* implies compulsion, deportation, and fear, the fear of suddenly losing family, work, education, your life! My greatest source of fear was the unknown on the other side of the border, Afghanistan itself, a country that in my mind was another name for war and bloodshed. This was what I often heard about Afghanistan from the media. Sometimes I imagined Afghanistan through the stories of my parents as a remote village somewhere in Daykundi—a mountainous area with long, cold winters, pleasant summers, and refreshing springs of cold water. At the same time, poverty, suffering, and war were the dominant themes of the stories we heard from the mountains.

Contrary to the concept common to migration studies of the 'myth of return', I don't recall my parents expressing a desire or longing to return to Afghanistan. In their conversations, return was more often mentioned as a threat and a source of worry. My father passed away in Mashhad in 2017, having lived approximately four decades of his life as an Afghan-Hazara migrant in Iran. He had lived in Iran more years than he had in Afghanistan. He had worked in Iran more than he had in Afghanistan, dug channels for telecommunications, gas, and sewage with his shovel and pickaxe, helped to build many buildings, and contributed to the prosperity of the city, yet he was not allowed to be a citizen of that city. In Iran, access to citizenship is extremely limited and in practice inaccessible for most Afghans.[2] As an Afghan-Hazara migrant, he had very limited job options, limitations that were enshrined in law in Iran. We were seen as uninvited guests in society, unwelcome guests-workers!

In 2008, despite having graduated from university, I couldn't envision a future for myself in Iran as an Afghan-Hazara-forced migrant. I considered moving to Afghanistan. The serious idea of moving to Afghanistan began when some of my friends, after graduating from universities, went to Afghanistan through the Return and Reintegration of Qualified and Skilled Afghan Nationals from the Islamic Republic of Iran to the Islamic Republic of Afghanistan (RRQSA) programme, facilitated by the International Organisation for Migration (IOM). This initiative is designed to encourage Afghans to 'return' to Afghanistan by finding placements for participants in either governmental or non-governmental private institutions, providing them with an eight-month temporary contract, including good salary provisions. I applied and was accepted for the programme in 2009. When I informed my father of my decision to move to Afghanistan for work, he didn't say anything. He neither encouraged nor discouraged me. But it was clear from his face that he was worried. At that time, nearly three decades had passed since he had left Afghanistan, and it was likely that much had changed (politically, socially, economically), especially since Afghanistan had once again come to international attention after 2001 and the defeat of the Taliban. But he was still worried, and I couldn't quite grasp why or why he himself had no desire to return!

The name of the programme sending me to Afghanistan intrigued me: Return and Reintegration of Qualified and Skilled Afghan Nationals from I.R Iran to I.R. Afghanistan. I grappled with the terms 'return' and 'reintegration.' 'Return' didn't seem right to us—many of our generation had been raised or born in Iran. Some of us had never been to Afghanistan, and some of us had grown up in Iran with no memories of Afghanistan. Thus, going to Afghanistan felt more like a new exile than a 'return', more like 'integration' rather than 'reintegration.' For me, everything was new, as if I was migrating to a new country.

After crossing the border, as soon as the taxi filled with five passengers, we started heading towards Herat and the sound of music was turned up. It was Ahmad Zahir, one of the few Afghan singers I knew. I had listened to this music over and over again working in carpet-weaving and tailoring workshops in Iran when I was a child. Listening to Afghan music with an Afghan driver and Afghan passengers in Afghanistan was delightful, something I hadn't heard in the public sphere in Iran during my lifetime there! All of this awakened a comforting feeling in me that I had never experienced in Iran, yet I was very cautious at the same time, as the environment was foreign to me. I had mostly lived in ghetto-like neighbourhoods like Golshahr on the outskirts of cities dominated by Hazara people like me, and I had little interaction with or understanding of the other ethnic groups in Afghanistan, only a vague impression formed from the internal wars in my mind, a hostile impression!

Upon entering Jebrael, another ghetto-like marginalised neighbourhood on the edge of Herat city in Western Afghanistan, I felt a greater sense of familiarity and comfort. Jebrael was a township established by Hazara displaced within Afghanistan and return-ees from Iran. Most of my friends who had returned from Iran had settled around the major cities of Kabul, Herat, and Mazar. No one was returning to their villages in the central regions of Afghanistan. The harsh nature, scarce and infertile lands, and suc-cessive droughts had put the few remaining inhabitants of the Hazara villages at risk (in Bamiyan, Daykundi, Ghor, and Ghazni), forcing some to migrate to and settle in the outskirts of the big cities in search of work.

The increase in the Hazara returnee and internally displaced population in some cities, like Herat, was always accompanied by tension and conflict with the host community. Later due to my job as a researcher, I had the chance to travel to different provinces and converse with a variety of people. In 2011, dur-ing a visit to Herat, I chatted with a local identifying himself as a native Herati. He voiced his concerns regarding the influx of 'migrants' and 'non-native' residents in Herat. He drew a clear line between 'us' and 'them,' referring to the newcomers as 'migrants' and 'non-natives' who predominantly resided along the outskirts of the city in settlements like Jebreal. He viewed their presence as a potential threat to the cultural and demographic fabric of Herat, an area with a majority Tajik population and old history and bright civilization. This 'othering' and racialization of dis-placed Hazara wasn't new to me, as I had often heard about this hostility from friends and family living in Herat's suburbs.

My destination was Kabul. Kabul was a unique and different place. Despite its dusty and dirty streets, it was full of life and activity. It felt like you could meet people from all over the world there, including every Afghan ethnic group. Besides those who had come from remote Afghan villages, there were people who had come back from Pakistan and Iran. They were now joined by foreigners from places as far away as America, Europe, Africa, Asia, and Australia. By comparison, Iran seemed much more homogenous than Kabul, which had really turned into a world city, full of diversity that was both new and exciting to me. The city was filled with the loud music of happy Indian and Afghan songs, something you wouldn't find in Iran. It was amazing to see how, after years of war and hardship, music could still be so powerful, bringing life and energy to the community. The bright and happy clothes worn by both women and men were really uplifting, reminding me of Bollywood films.

In Kabul's streets and alleys, people spoke Farsi with a Kabuli accent, but there were many different Farsi accents present: Panjshiri, Badakhshani, Bamyani, Kandahari, and Herati. Also, in some offices in Kabul, you could hear foreigners with different English accents, including American, British, New Zealand, and Australian, as well as English spoken with French and Italian accents. I had no trouble understanding people or making myself understood in Farsi; I could understand almost all the accents. Even though the Kabuli accent was seen as the standard and was everywhere—in the streets, markets, and media—giving it more importance, the variety of languages in Kabul really showed how inclusive and international the city had become after years of continuous war and conflict.

This diversity of people, accents, and languages created a good feeling in me. I felt satisfied to have left Iran and come to diverse Kabul. I was happy to have found work through my education, feeling valuable and useful, but most importantly, I had become hopeful about the future. I could think about the future, dream, something that had been denied to me in Iran. What could be more important than that for a person who had lived his life as a migrant with all sorts of limitations? This happiness and hope made the lack of amenities less bothersome. In Kabul, we usually didn't have electricity at night or even during the day, the noise of generators was nerve-wracking, the streets were full of dust in the summer and mud in the winter, there was no drinking water, and public health standards were not observed, but I was increasingly focused on the future. I was happy to play a role in the rebuilding of Afghanistan.

Accent, identity, and power

My first day at work started with meeting the IOM team in Kabul to introduce me to my workplace in one of the government departments in Kabul. Walking into the IOM office in Kabul was a surprise. After spending a few days in the vibrant and diverse city of Kabul, the office seemed homogeneous. Everyone I met was Pashtun and spoke Pashto between themselves, which I couldn't understand. I looked around for some familiar faces but found no one. The IOM office didn't represent Kabul's diverse character. This big difference in diversity between the city life and IOM office was disappointing. It wasn't a good sign.

Accompanied by an employee from the IOM office, we went to my workplace. I was introduced to the head and a few colleagues. Again, the diversity that I had seen in the streets and alleys of Kabul was absent. The group was relatively uniform, though this time most spoke Farsi. The colleagues were mostly

Tajik. Yet again, I searched for a Hazara face, but there were only two others who, like me, had recently come to Kabul from Iran through the IOM programme. The Hazara features and Farsi accent distinguished us from our other colleagues. Our accent was not entirely Irani (Tehrani, Mashhadi...), not entirely Kabuli, and not entirely Hazaragi. It bore signs of all these, yet it was none of them, it was/is a distinct accent reflecting our mobility.

Our salary was approximately six times higher than that of a regular government employee starting their career in the public sector. The same programme by IOM was also accessible to Afghans residing in Europe, encouraging their participation in the reconstruction of Afghanistan. Their salaries were five times higher than ours, and they had their European passport, which would allow them to return to Europe whenever they liked. This salary difference had created a kind of resentment among the other employees towards us in the department. In addition, we had not endured the hardships and sufferings of the war, had fled Afghanistan to Iran, had the chance to study abroad although with difficulty, and now had 'returned' to Afghanistan as qualified and skilled Afghan nationals. Often, the struggles and hardships of forced migration were overlooked by those who had never left Afghanistan.

I soon realised that in Kabul, with its vast diversity of people and accents, my mixed accent was deemed less legitimate and was sometimes challenged at work and in public as an 'Iranian accent'. In public spaces, I could feel the disapproving looks and comments from others, which was unpleasant. We were accused of losing our 'Afghan' culture and identity and adopting an alien culture and accent. A label often used for returnees from Iran was *Iranigak* which literally means little Iranian, usually meant in a mocking and derogatory way. Gradually, in public spaces, I took more care to speak with a Kabuli accent and avoid speaking in a mixed accent or Iranian accent and tried not to use Farsi words common in Iran but not in Afghanistan. My friend Ahmad, a Hazara who returned from Iran and was working on a contract basis in a ministry, listened to *Khane-Naw, Zendegi-Naw* ('New Home, New Life'), a programme on BBC Persian radio, and would repeat sentences after the presenter to learn the Kabuli accent. However, sometimes it didn't work. He once told me that during a disagreement over a fare with a taxi driver, he remarked, 'No problem, I'll get another *Mashin*' (car in Iranian Farsi). The driver mockingly responded, 'Go get another *Mashin*,' sneering as he echoed the term. In Afghanistan, the word for car is *motar*.

Beyond the streets and markets and into the media, we witnessed similar experiences. In 2009, on the 'Afghan Star' singing competition, Elaha Soroor, a Hazara Iran-born returnee girl, participated. For her audition, she sang a song called 'Sultan-e Qalbha' by the Iranian singer Aref, in the style of Ahmad Zahir, the famous Afghan singer. Her Iranian accent was clearly noticeable. She was told by one of the Pashtun judges with his accented Farsi, 'Sing an Afghan song, whatever it is, just make sure it's Afghan.' Elaha tried to sing an Afghan song, but her accent tended to revert to Iranian accent while singing. Once again, the judge scolded her: 'Whenever you sing, do not sing with an Iranian accent, only sing with an Afghan accent', yet singing in Hindi was tolerated. Interestingly, despite all the challenges, Elaha Soroor managed to reach 8th place in Afghan Star in 2009, which was a significant achievement for a Hazara girl who had returned from Iran. Now she lives abroad and has become a professional singer.

Our mixed accent, which in Iran could sometimes act as a protective shield against hostility and violence in the host society, had become a tool for exposure to hostility and violence at 'home', in Kabul. In both societies, I learned (tried to speak) with another accent (Kabuli, Mashhadi, Tehrani) more for protection and legitimacy rather than assimilation or integration. Protecting against potential dangers, safeguarding against verbal violence, and shielding from demeaning glances were all important measures against a dominant and hostile society. However, these efforts were often in vain, as our distinct physical Hazaragi features set us apart from the dominant members of society (Iranians in Iran and Pashtuns and Tajiks in Afghanistan). Accent was highly hierarchical and intertwined with ethnicity and power in Afghanistan history.

The Iranian accent in Hazara returnees from Iran sometimes limited their access to resources and job opportunities in contrast to those who returned from Europe or America. Ahmad, who had become fluent in the Kabuli accent after several years, mentioned that there was a debate in the ministry he worked for about giving a job to a returnee from Iran. Despite his high skills and qualifications, the ministry's leadership was reluctant to place him in the position because it was a public relations position that attracted media attention and there were still faint traces of an Iranian accent in his speech. Additionally, there were concerns that his accent could have been suspicious or questionable to some American donors too, given the hostile relations between Iran and the US.

The presence of American military forces in Afghanistan was perceived as a threat by Iran, which shares about 900 kilometres of border with Afghanistan. Iran was under sanctions imposed by the United States, and as a result, Afghanistan's trade and political dealings with Iran were approached with increased caution and scrutiny. American donors in Afghanistan explicitly stated that no Iranian goods should be purchased with American funds in Afghanistan.

In this setting, the Iranian accent of the so-called *Iranigaks*, regardless of its cultural and social dimensions as a consequence of migration, was understood in an entirely political context. The Iranian accent of Hazara returnees was perceived as a continuation of the ideological influence of Iran's Shia rule in Afghanistan. Linking Hazaras to Iran was used strategically to suppress their political movements in Afghanistan, such as the *Roshanaee*[3] (Enlightenment) movement in 2016. Even nowadays, some Hazara political leaders and intellectuals are concerned about being linked to Iran by Pashtun and Tajik political leaders in Afghanistan. This concern persists even though Hazara people (and Tajiks and Pashtuns) migrate to Iran for pilgrimage and work, a pattern that has existed for centuries. This political misuse by dominant political ethnic groups is problematic. Iran, as an ideologically Shia, Farsi speaking country, is mistrusted in Afghanistan, a predominantly Sunni country governed by Pashto speakers, and was always under suspicion, especially in a country under the influence of the US and Europe.

As a result, these accents, along with other cultural markers like clothing, food, and music, born from the Hazaras' forced migration to Iran, were not trusted. Instead, they were viewed as signs of political loyalty to Iran and as a drifting away from Afghan culture. This perspective served as a basis for a new layer of discrimination by the more dominant groups, effectively leading to Hazaras being racially categorised upon our return from Iran. Accents, in this context, took on a political dimension far beyond the usual consequences of migration, becoming entangled in the larger geopolitical tensions and domestic power struggles within Afghanistan.

Furthermore, Hazara returnees from Iran who spoke with a Hazaragi accent found themselves lacking in perceived legitimacy within the public sphere and were often subject to ridicule. The long-standing history of discrimination against Hazaras had pushed the Hazaragi accent into a private sphere, such that when used in public settings, it was deemed insufficiently legitimate for interaction and consequently marginalised. Against this backdrop, the act of speaking in a Hazaragi accent and the public embrace of Hazara cultural symbols effectively became a form of resistance against their marginalisation.

The presence of Hazaras, especially those returning from Iran with a distinct accent, was hard to digest within the system, as historically, Hazaras had been conspicuously absent from both governmental and non-governmental institutions. Our emergence, especially in senior roles within these institutions, represented a departure from dominant traditional, social, and political norms, making their acceptance difficult and subject to scrutiny. The assembly of several Hazaras in a single office space was often met with suspicion and provoked questions and sensitivities, contrasting sharply with the unremarked and normalised presence of other ethnic groups in similar settings, which aligned with the established historical, social, and political expectations and did not invite suspicion.

In 2014, I was working at a non-governmental organisation within a research institute focusing on human rights. I was one of the senior employees and usually participated in job interviews. For one of the positions, the most suitable candidate based on meritocracy was Hazara. After the interviews, one of the non-Hazara managers, a member of the interviewing panel, openly apologised to me and then stated that we should not hire more Hazaras, claiming we had enough Hazaras and that hiring more would create sensitivities and disrupt the ethnic balance. Such a perspective was a result of the deep-rooted historical bias in the minds of individuals within Afghan society against Hazaras.

During a stay at a non-Hazara friend's house in Kabul, an evening conversation with his father brought up the common question of my origins in Afghanistan, a detail deeply intertwined with one's identity. Upon learning I was from Daykundi, a province predominantly inhabited by Hazaras, he remarked on the hard-working nature of its people. This observation, while intended as a compliment, resonated differently with me. Despite hearing similar remarks even in London, the label 'hardworking' carried a bittersweet undertone for Hazaras, more reflecting a history of systemic deprivation than a positive trait.

The perception of Hazaras as hardworking is rooted in their historical exclusion from higher education and government roles, relegating many to menial labour in Kabul's markets—a testament to their resilience in the face of discrimination. Within my circle, it's rare to find anyone whose relatives were part of the governmental or non-governmental sectors, academia, or national media. This gap in our collective history poses a profound question for the current generation of Hazaras, highlighting a legacy of exclusion and the ongoing journey towards inclusion and recognition.

National labels

When I was in Iran, I got tired of anything labelled 'national'— I resented it. The term 'national' made me question my identity every day and reminded me I didn't belong. Sadly, in Iran, lots of things were tagged with 'national'. The national anthem, national ID, national car, national park, National Bank, National Library, National Iranian Oil Company, National Iranian Gas Company, national production, national team, even national shoes, everything was branded as national and, of course, Islamic. 'National' was an exclusionary term, and Afghan forced migrants were positioned as outsiders, a potential threat to this 'national' integrity and disruptive of it.

I recall, whenever the Iranian national football team played, I found myself automatically supporting the other team. It felt like Iran was my opponent. Particularly during matches against South Korea, Japan, or China, I somehow saw a reflection of myself in their almond-shaped eyes, even though that was the only thing we had in common. Those same almond eyes that always caused us trouble in Iran. The racialisation of Afghan forced migrants in Iran is manifested through the physical appearance of Hazaras who are exposed to overt racism, discrimination, and physical attacks, while for other Afghan ethnic groups (Tajik and

Pashtun), their facial features, similar to those of Iranians, are a protective shield.

When I went to Afghanistan, my issue with national suffixes intensified. In Afghanistan, the problem was that I couldn't understand most of the national things because they were in the Pashto language. The national ID card was in Pashto, the national currency had inscriptions in Pashto, and the national anthem was in Pashto. I didn't know the national anthem and didn't feel any connection to it because I couldn't see myself in it. During ceremonies when the national anthem was played, I would silently observe my colleagues who would sometimes hum the anthem with pride and joy. Playing the national anthem at the start of events was common in Afghanistan, often interpreted as patriotism. I participated in this display, playing my role in silence. Either I was not part of the nation or the anthem wasn't national. I had become sceptical of all things labelled national. The national things challenged and denied me in different ways both in Iran and Afghanistan. I (a Hazara Shia Farsi Speaker) was also disrupting the dominant national order in both countries.

One day in 2012, I went to the Ministry of Finance in Kabul for an interview for a research project. I was supposed to interview a young woman who worked in a high position at the Ministry of Finance. I didn't know Pashto, and she didn't understand Farsi, so we began to speak in English. She spoke English with an American accent, while my English was broken. Both of us were discussing significant national issues of Afghanistan in a non-national language. We were speaking the language of donors, which was more important and powerful than the national languages in Afghanistan. She had become a compatriot and co-linguist through migration to the donor countries. Probably, when my parents migrated to Iran, her parents had migrated to the West as they might have had better resources.

Returnees from Western countries with Western passports in their pocket, often secured better job opportunities and commanded higher salaries, leading to resentment among Afghans who had endured the difficulties of decades of conflict. These Afghans found themselves with only a minimal portion of the international aid and investment entering the country on their behalf. In a derogatory fashion, those who had returned from the West were pejoratively termed *Sag Shoi* (dog washer). As dogs are considered **najes** (ritually impure) in Islamic tradition, the label implied that these returnees had engaged in menial or demeaning tasks in the West.

Kabul became a hub for numerous international NGOs, which sought returnee or local employees fluent in English. As a result, learning English became a widespread pursuit, transcending its practical utility to become a benchmark for assessing an individual's knowledge and skills. In this environment, the concept of *Khareji*, denoting a foreigner or outsider, assumed a status of prestige and desirability, specifically referring to individuals from affluent Western nations. Iranians and Pakistanis did not fit into this category of *Khareji*. Typically, the ideal *Khareji* was imagined as someone white, with blond hair and blue eyes, setting a standard that marginalised other foreigners as less important. This distinction underscored the complex dynamics of global influence and local perceptions in Afghanistan.

In 2011, I travelled to Nangarhar province in eastern Afghanistan with a work team to collect data for a research project. I was in charge of the team, having trained them for data collection and conducting interviews. People in Jalalabad spoke Pashto, and few knew Farsi, which frustrated me as I struggled to communicate with the locals. However, I accompanied kind and friendly Pashtun colleagues in the field during the interviews, dressed in traditional attire as usual. A Pashto-speaking colleague approached a bakery to conduct an interview when the baker upon seeing me left his oven and rushed towards me, starting to speak in English: 'Hello, how are you?' Surprised, I responded with a smile and in English, 'I'm fine, how are you?' Suddenly, my colleague burst into laughter and said: 'He isn't *Khareji*, he is Afghan.' Although my appearance didn't closely resemble that of a 'standard' *Khareji*, the baker had assumed I might be from East Asia due to the absence of Hazaras in that area and was excited to see me in his bakery.

Besides English, which was considered the primary power in the hierarchical language system, many jobs in Afghanistan required proficiency in the national languages (Pashto and Farsi). Priority was given to those who were fluent in both national languages. Pashto, more than being a communicative necessity in the workplace in Kabul, had become a technique for excluding Farsi speakers from job opportunities. Those of us who had returned from Iran were automatically disqualified from many jobs because we did not know Pashto, the more 'national' language. Pashto was part of the curriculum in primary and higher education in Afghanistan, and Farsi speakers who had been educated in Afghanistan were familiar with Pashto to a basic extent, enough to fit into the dominant national order and have a better chance of employment than those of us educated in Iran.

My friend Karim, a Hazara returnee from Iran who had studied English literature in Iran and had a high proficiency in English, had started learning Pashto because he had lost a good job opportunity at an international organisation solely because he didn't know Pashto. It was fascinating to me how, over two decades (2001–2021), everyone tried to find a way to bypass the Pashto language barrier in job interviews. For example, one recommendation was to always write in the CV under the Pashto language skills section: 'Currently learning Pashto.' Sometimes, this expressed interest in learning the more 'national' language solved the problem. Some Pashtun employers were satisfied just seeing us trying to become more 'national.' Sadeq, who didn't know Pashto, in a job interview, when asked about his Pashto proficiency, started singing in Pashto. He had memorised one of the songs by a famous Pashto singer. It was effective—the panel members were pleased, and he got the job.

National ID (Tazkera)

With rage and in a Hazaragi accent, he shouted: 'Aren't we citizens of this country? If we are not considered citizens, then tell us we are not! If we are, then why won't you solve the problem and give me the National ID?' Then, with even-greater anger, he yelled: 'I don't even want this National ID anymore!' The tired and angry old man tore up his National ID application and the attached documents, throwing them towards the sky. The National ID office worker was taken aback by the old man's fury, seemingly not expecting it and slightly shocked.

In my heart, I admired him; how bravely he had stepped forward with his Hazaragi accent, striking right at the heart of the matter with honesty and courage: 'Aren't we citizens of this country?' Even years later, every time I face discrimination and prejudice his words still resonate in my mind with that Hazaragi accent. Usually, those of us who came from Iran became prey to the corruption in Afghan bureaucratic systems, and with our mixed (Mashhadi, Tehrani, Hazaragi, Kabuli) accents, we did not dare to protest—we were more likely to compromise. How could one protest in Kabul, the capital of Afghanistan, with a Mashhadi or Tehrani accent? It wasn't legitimate enough.

Ali's Mashhadi accent was noticeable. When applying for a National ID card and speaking Farsi with a mix of Kabul and Mashhadi accents, he was treated with mistrust and suspicion. His father had migrated to Iran 40 years ago and had passed away there a few years before, without a National ID card. Ali's elderly mother also did not have a National ID card. Ali had lost contact with his relatives and kin in Afghanistan long ago. He knew no one, having only recently arrived in Afghanistan. To obtain a National ID card, he needed to find a National ID card of a father, uncle, brother, or close first-degree male relative and, in addition, find two currently employed government workers who could testify they knew him and confirm his residency in a specific city, village, or town. Many of us did not know anyone in Afghanistan, let alone have government employees as acquaintances.

We had just arrived and still did not understand the language and the relationships governing Afghan institutions. A good network or money solved all administrative and national issues in Afghanistan, but we had neither such a network nor had we accumulated enough money during the years of migration. Therefore, we became easy prey in the corrupt administrative environment of Afghanistan, searching for national documents to prove that we are Afghan nationals and establish our lives and homes in Afghanistan.

Fluid spaces and identity

At home in Kabul, I sometimes listened to Iranian music, read books published in Iran, and enjoyed some Iranian dishes. Occasionally, I watched Iranian movies and series or films with Iranian dubbing. At home, we spoke in our mixed Farsi accent, but outdoors, we tried to speak more in the Kabuli accent.

Gradually, in the 2010s beyond the private spaces of our homes, in the Pul-e-Sorkh area of Kabul, restaurants serving Iranian cuisine began to emerge, such as *Nan-e Dagh Kabab Dagh*, *Negin Asia*, and *Khalifa Avaz*, all offering dishes with Iranian flavours. Iranian sweets and traditional ice cream were also available. Many bookstores had opened, primarily selling books printed in Iran by Iranian authors and translators. As cafes were established, they became gathering spots for *Iranigaks*, where people sipped green and black tea and coffee, discussing everything from migration, art, literature, discrimination, corruption, to suicide bombings. Occasionally, in the evenings, I would go to the traditional restaurant *Maiwand*, and hangout with my friends (often with experience of living in Iran), to drink tea and share stories. Although the spaces created in Pul-e-Sorkh carried some cultural symbols of Iran and were labelled as *Iranigak*, the perception of Iran in those spaces was extremely negative. Most Hazara people with lived experiences in Iran had largely bitter memories of life there, were averse to Iran's ideological atmosphere, and felt a sense of solidarity with Iranian dissidents and members of the arts and literature community who criticised the current conditions in Iran.

Despite the bitterness of migration in Iran, one of the most significant achievements of the Hazara diaspora was the educated individuals who returned to Afghanistan, revitalising the cultural and educational landscape in western Kabul and throughout Afghanistan, even though they were largely excluded from political and economic power. Around Pul-e-Sorkh in Kabul, private universities were established by Hazara returnees from Iran. I, too, taught part-time at some of these universities. In these universities, lecturers were not forced to disguise our hybrid accents, which posed less of a challenge even for non-Hazara students. These professors, who often struggled to overcome the corrupt and discriminatory hiring processes at Kabul's public universities, succeeded in creating their own educational and cultural spaces around Pul-e-Sorkh. The demand for such education was very high, attracting many young people from more distant provinces to Kabul, Herat, and Mazar for their studies.

My friend Davood, who held a doctoral degree in social science from Iran and was a senior lecturer at one of these private universities, had applied for an academic position at Kabul University. A non-Hazara senior lecturer from Kabul University, who only had a bachelor's degree, conducted his job interview. Ultimately, he was not accepted for the position at Kabul University for reasons that were unclear to him, but we all knew that the underlying reason was the usual discrimination against Hazaras, especially those who had returned from Iran. Ironically, several years later, when the first master's courses were offered at this private university, that same Kabul University senior lecturer attended classes taught by the same Davood who he had rejected from Kabul University.

In liminal places like Pul-e-Surkh in Kabul and Golshahr in Mashhad, national identity boundaries blur, leading to the emergence of a new space that is neither fully Afghan nor entirely Iranian. Instead, it embodies elements of both while remaining distinct from each. Identities in such spaces are fluid but constantly face challenges amid the struggles of nationalist powers that branded some identities as national and others non-national. These hybrid identities are often seen as a threat and typically marginalised and perceived as outside the conventional national and patriotic norms.

Re-migration

From 2015, there was an alarming surge in suicide bombings and explosive attacks targeting the Hazara community, a trend that persists into 2024 under the Taliban. The improved security trumpeted by the Taliban regime does not extend to Hazara communities. These attacks have occurred in schools, educational centres, places of worship, hospitals, sports centres, cultural and commercial centres, voter registration sites, protest gatherings, and public transportation, especially in Hazara-dominated areas, notably in western Kabul. These attacks did not target any specific military, political, cultural category, or age or gender group;

simply being Hazara, regardless of any category, is enough to be targeted. It is a Hazara genocide (Hakimi, 2023).

The continuous explosions disrupted the daily lives of Hazara people, filling commuting with fear and caution. Whenever I used public transportation, I thought about explosions and death. This fear of being blown up accompanied me in all public spaces. The Islamic Republic of Afghanistan's government failed to protect the Hazaras and did not show a serious desire to stop the attacks.

In 2016, tired of the discrimination we faced and the disheartening social atmosphere, filled with corruption and violence in the political landscape, I posted a poem by Langston Hughes, the African American poet, translated by Ahmad Shamlou, the Iranian poet, on Facebook. Shamlou had replaced 'America' with 'homeland' in his translation, and for me it referred to the fragile situation in Afghanistan and expressed the desire for this country to truly be our homeland:

> Let my homeland be the dream the dreamers
> dreamed—
> Let it be that great strong land of love
> Where never kings connive nor tyrants scheme
> That any man be crushed by one above.
> (It never was a homeland to me.)
> O, let my land be a land where Liberty
> Is crowned with no false patriotic wreath,
> But opportunity is real, and life is free,
> Equality is in the air we breathe.
> (There's never been equality for me,
> Nor freedom in this "homeland of the free.")

English translation of Shamlu's adaptation (1984)
of Langston Hughes' America never was America
to me

And I too had wished to let this homeland be a homeland for me, for all Hazara. A former colleague commented under my post, 'You have a homeland, your homeland is Iran'. In the aftermath of each suicide attack targeting the Hazara community, the idea of leaving Afghanistan weighed heavily on my mind. The fear that a tragedy might strike my family haunted me, stirring worries that I would be consumed by self-blame if any harm came to them. However, the prospect of migrating back to Iran, where our extended families resided, was no longer an option we considered. I was determined to find pathways to Western countries instead. To return to Iran would feel like stepping back into a past I had struggled to move beyond, a sentiment none of us wished to revisit.

In 2021, when the Taliban took over the capital, I was living in a building with seven apartments. All the families had something in common: we had grown up in Iran as migrants, had been educated there, and then returned to Afghanistan. To make those difficult days a bit easier (from August 15 when they rolled into Kabul to my evacuation on August 19), we would gather together, all the while thinking about how to leave Afghanistan. Everyone was considering moving to the West. However, for many people, moving to Iran remained the only possible choice for survival, despite the discrimination humiliation, and restrictive policies they would face.

With the Taliban's control over the country, conditions for minority groups like the Hazaras worsened, involving arrests, removals from offices, and forced relocations to seize Hazara lands. Furthermore, widespread unemployment and poverty have led to a significant number of people migrating towards Pakistan and Iran.

Evacuated from Afghanistan to Poland on August 19, 2021, I subsequently moved to the UK to finish my doctoral studies that had started in 2020. While living in Afghanistan, I struggled to forge a bond with the concept of a homeland. This detachment was deeply rooted in my experiences and interactions within Afghanistan. While living in Iran as an Afghan migrant, my perception of homeland was shaped, mainly as a response to the discrimination I faced there.

I gradually came to understand my father's silence about returning to Afghanistan and his lack of interest in living there. His apprehension stemmed from enduring the prejudices of being Hazara in Afghanistan. Despite the passage of time, the fall of multiple governments, and the rise of new ones, certain realities remained unchanged. The bias against Hazaras persisted, underscoring a continuity amidst change.

5
Continuous mobility: Pains and possibilities

Khadija Abbasi

English breakfast

Oh, how winter nights are long in the UK! My window had no curtain, and I could see how the sunlight was pushing its way out through the grey sky that looked lower than usual. Day was coming very reluctantly. My elderly roommate was quietly sleeping. From behind, she could look like my mother or maybe I was looking for similarities between her and my mother who was so far away from me. She slowly woke up and prepared for morning prayers. She limped towards the bathroom, and I did not want to think how she was going to perform Wudu and wash her feet in this Western style bathroom. She limped back and threw her praying mat and herself to the floor and started praying while seated. Watching her praying and looking upward toward the low ceiling was comforting. The humming of Arabic prayers felt so familiar and soothing. I wish I knew some Arabic and could ask her to pray for me. How come those endless Arabic lessons at schools in Iran never worked for me! My mother would pray if she knew where I was, but God forbid. How could I tell her I am in a prison? How could she bear the pain of imagining her only daughter in prison? How could I explain to her that all my hard work to come to Europe was to end up so disrespectfully in a detention centre? I remembered how at Kabul airport when we separated as I left for London to study, I looked back at her for the last time to say a final farewell and noticed she had turned back to secretly wipe away her tears. She did not want me to see her tears and I did not want to cause her pain. I enjoyed watching my roommate praying, but I did not have the will to stand and pray myself. Those days I was revisiting and negotiating my relationship with Islam.

Finally, the clock struck 7am and it was time for breakfast. My roommate had gone back to sleep and did not seem to be ready to go downstairs for some unfamiliar breakfast. She was not able to walk well, it was too painful to go to the bathroom, let alone going to the canteen. That morning, I decided to bring her some dry food. I remembered that there were white toasts and thin slices of cheese. I could make one or two Halal sandwiches for her. I thought I would be the first in the canteen, but I realised many women like me could not wait to get out of their room. I ate my breakfast and prepared a few toasts for my roommate and wrapped them in paper towels. I tried to imagine her happy face after receiving food and that made me excited. While I was going up the stairs, a male young white member of the staff saw me and asked me what I was carrying in the towel. It was obvious that it was food, but I told him what it was. He asked me to unwrap and show him. He said it is against their internal regulations to carry food and consume it in our room. I explained that it is for my elderly roommate who cannot walk well. He insisted that she has to come down herself and I must put back the food. He was a few steps higher than me. A white man intimidating a brown woman. I felt like a maid who had stolen food for her poor family. Did he really believe me? Was he really thinking that I was stealing food? Was that breakfast really worth stealing? Was he really trying to respect the regulation or did he want to show me his little power? Had he ever tasted our breakfasts? Does he know back in Iran and Afghanistan we eat freshly baked bread for breakfast which cannot be compared with these industrially made white toasts? The unseasoned scrambled eggs on white toast in the canteen was good, but for me it was not as tasty as eggs cooked with fresh tomatoes and onions, seasoned with local spices and served with cardamom flavoured green tea. I went back to the canteen to put back the food. Nobody would use those sandwiches anyway, so I had to throw them in the bin. I felt terrible. I felt disrespected and humiliated.

Yarl's wood immigration removal centre

I arrived at the Yarl's Wood removal centre in March 2008. Yarl's Wood is the largest immigration removal centre for women in the UK. The private security company Serco has been responsible for managing it since 2007. Three categories of people are detained in this centre: foreign nationals who have served a sentence in the UK and await deportation, asylum seekers like me who were waiting for processing of their asylum application, and those who have entered or remained in the country illegally.

Figure 5.1 © Copyright Oliver White and licensed for reuse under Creative Commons Licence

Upon arrival, I went through a round of security checks. All of my belongings were confiscated. I did not have much with me anyway. I only had my LSE-logoed backpack with me containing my laptop and the mobile phone that one of my brothers had gifted me and a few bank notes. My laptop and the sim card of my mobile phone were taken away, and I was only allowed to use my mobile with the new sim card the prison authorities provided. That was enough for me to be connected to the outside world through my partner who was based in India and found ways to put credit in my phone so that we could keep in touch and work on my asylum application.

I was put in a room with a disabled elderly woman from Sudan who had mobility restrictions. There were two beds and a bathroom in the room. The bathroom was not suitable for an elderly person and that might be the reason she had not taken a shower for a long time. Her English was very limited, and we hardly could have a meaningful conversation. I managed to make her understand that I was born in Iran, hoping our shared religion would create a common ground. She rightfully associated Iran with Ayatullah Khomeini and guessed that I might be a Shia Muslim and lost any interest in listening to me. I should have mentioned Afghanistan instead!

Before my arrival at this centre, and during my initial screening interview at the Home Office in Croydon, south London, the officer in charge asked me whether I had any legal representation. I did not. The officer recommended that I find one before my main interview. Through a friend, I found details of an organisation that provided free legal advice to asylum seekers. That organisation is closed now. When I arrived at this removal centre, my partner, the lawyer, and I started working together to compile any necessary documents that would strengthen my case. My lawyer had warned me seriously that most people in this removal centre, as the name suggests, get removed back to their country of origin. The shock of arriving in a prison had not settled down and I now had to deal with the stress of getting deported back to Afghanistan.

There was a possibility of being bailed out, but I could not afford the amount required and I also could not find anyone who would pay for this. We were all confined indoors and the only way to get fresh air was to open our windows, but these were secured and could not be opened wide. My window was facing a brick wall which was 2 meters away and I could see a tiny bit of sky. Most of the women in the prison were brown or black. The dynamics, strength, and positivity that black women brought with them in that rather depressing building has stayed in my mind vividly. The resistance of these women in keeping the prison a lively place gave me some strength to hold myself up. I remember there was a room which looked like a hair salon. I never stepped into it. I wish I was not isolated and could enter, but the sound of life and laughter coming from that room made this place less like a prison.

I never disclosed the experience of this removal centre to my family, particularly to my parents who have now departed from this world. They would be devastated to know their daughter was imprisoned. People of Afghanistan who have migrated try to portray a successful image of themselves in the West to families left back in Afghanistan. I wanted my family to know that they made the right decision to support my departure to Europe. I did not want to look like a loser. I was still in this undeclared mission of proving to myself and my family that I can look after myself as a single woman. In addition, I did not want to give them a hard time as they were not able to do anything for me from afar. However, the women in the prison looked after one another. A young woman from Sierra Leone was particularly kind to me. We were both in the same car when we arrived at this removal centre. I was not keen to socialise simply because I was trying to understand what was going on around me. She brought me out of my dark moments by making me dance to the songs she sang beautifully. One day, in her room she told me her story and pulled up her T-shirt to show me the signs of torture on her body. It was very confusing and shocking that both of us felt we needed protection as our lives were at risk in our country of origin, but the asylum system in the UK rejected us.

Towards the west

The fall of the Taliban in 2001 had created a sense of optimism in Afghanistan. Hundreds of local and international non-governmental organisations and UN agencies had popped up in Afghanistan. There was an exciting mood of 'reconstruction' in the air. However, the optimism did not last long. Afghanistan was becoming increasingly dangerous. Taliban insurgencies had reappeared. The actual fighting with the NATO forces mainly took place in the south and southeast parts of Afghanistan, but the fighting was gradually spreading to other areas of Afghanistan. NATO forces were supposedly fighting to bring lasting peace and development to Afghanistan and liberate women from Afghan men and a patriarchal society. But for many, including the Taliban, US-led forces were considered foreign occupying forces imposing a hegemonic Western ideology. The 'civilising mission' of the development regime was not working and was instead adding more tension to the communities that for a long time had been suffering from many political and economic upheavals. The donors' obsession with 'gender mainstreaming' was one of the elements that irritated many communities (men and women) whose main concerns were not increased public visibility of women, but poverty reduction, lack of health and education infrastructure, clean water, unemployment, insecurity, etc.

Thanks to a degree in English-Farsi translation that I had obtained in Iran, I could join a foreign NGO in late 2004, a few months after I was forced to leave Iran and saw Afghanistan for the first time. I worked for two years for this NGO. Around mid-2006, it was getting clear to the head of the NGO I was working with (a white Western man) in Mazar-e Sharif that my life was in danger, and I should leave his NGO. This came after my long struggle and resistance to some of my colleagues who had been pushing me for some time to resign. As an Iran-born and Iran-raised Hazara 'returnee' woman, some of my colleagues found my behaviour unacceptable. I had been living a delusion of making Afghanistan my home after a life in Iran and was fighting for my position on various grounds: trying to be a financially independent single woman at home; fighting for some freedom of movement in a new country; figuring out my way in a country I was forced unwillingly to adopt as a 'home country', and constructing my identity as a female Hazara citizen of Afghanistan, a country that had become infected with ethnic, religious, and linguistic tensions. In the meantime, at work with my colleagues, I had entered into another battle trying to prove that I was capable of doing the job I had been entrusted with—improving women's participation in the National Solidarity Programme. The status of being *Iranigak* had complicated my already minoritized and marginalised identity as a female Shia Hazara woman in a Sunni majority country run by Pashtun elites.

The rejection I encountered in Afghanistan was not unique to me. Millions who had returned to Afghanistan or visited for the very first-time experienced discrimination and marginalisation on various levels, as described by Reza in the previous chapter. In the same NGO, I developed feelings for a colleague (the partner who helped me while I was in detention and whom I married ten years later). Although our socialisation could only occur in public spaces such as the dining room of guest houses or on long drives to the fieldwork sites, I did not realise that I was still breaking some unwritten rules. This had caused discomfort among some of my male colleagues. In an email from a high ranking and elderly 'white-bearded' male colleague to the head of the NGO, I was accused of behaving like Iranian women who are not familiar with the culture of Afghanistan and causing disruption to the project. It was not the first and the last email pressure from colleagues to the head of the NGO. The head of the NGO suggested that I work in other branches in the region, such as Pakistan or Tajikistan. Instead, I resigned and thanks to a scholarship, I went to the UK to study for my master's degree.

I feared for my life when I left Afghanistan, but I looked at this journey as a way to get away from the crisis and instead focus on self-development. I therefore informed my family and colleagues that I am travelling to the UK not to save my life but to study for my master's degree. I did not take the decision to leave Afghanistan lightly. Growing up in an environment where immediate family and extended families and community play a key role in our daily socialisation, it was not easy for me to imagine myself all by myself in a completely new country. Similarly, it was not easy for my parents to see their young and single daughter travel abroad to study. My family had already had to deal with the pressure from our community to stop me from working for a foreign NGO. Many Afghans, including my family and relatives, looked at these foreign NGOs with suspicion. Despite these pressures, we had come to an agreement and I was able to work and contribute financially to my family.

Early one morning in summer 2006, when my father was performing his morning prayers outdoors next to our garden, I sat next to
him to discuss my departure to the UK. He had just finished and
was reciting Zikr with his praying beads. He was definitely enjoying those spiritual moments under the sky while warm breezes
were making our vine branches and sunflowers sway. My mother
was in the sleeping net trying to wake up my siblings for the
prayer. I told my father that a degree from the West would facilitate my integration into the Afghan government, a position he
always hoped for me. Many government officials of Afghanistan
had studied in the West. To be part of the government, for him,
meant to be part of the central power, he never enjoyed in
Afghanistan as a marginalised man. Since the persecution and
subjugation of the Hazaras in the late nineteenth century, lower
socio-economic status had marked the Hazara people's landscape. My father was a landless peasant who worked on other
people's lands until he found his way to Kabul to work as a porter.
He later started making trips to Iran for seasonal work, and in late
1970s, right after the Soviet invasion, he took his young family
with him to Iran and settled there.

That morning, he finally agreed with a heavy heart that I could
go and study in the UK and gave me his blessings. My elder
brother was not happy with the idea of me leaving home as a
single woman, but who could confront my father! That summer
of 2006 we had all planned to visit Daykundi for the very first
time with my parents. The province of Daykundi was the birthplace of my parents. For the first time since 1977 when they had
left for Iran, they were able to travel to their village, Quchanqi. My
father had lost his parents when he was child, but my mother was

around 16 years old when she had left her father and her home village for Iran, and now, she was going to visit his gravestone. Central Afghanistan is among the most impoverished parts of Afghanistan, and the village of my parents had not gone through many changes since they left.

But that summer, after gaining the approval of my parents, I had to travel to Pakistan to apply for the British visa as there was no British consulate in Afghanistan. I regret that I missed my once in a life-time chance to visit Daykundi with my parents. I do not know how much I can know about that precious piece of land without the presence of my deceased parents. Above all, I wanted to visit Daykundi for a symbolic reason. It is my official and adopted place of birth, since neither Iranian nor Afghan authorities were willing to put Iran as my birthplace on my identification documents. Now, the Taliban has taken over the country, there is no way for me to visit Afghanistan, let alone Daykundi.

Life in the UK as student

Despite fearing for my life, when I arrived in the UK, I did not think of claiming for asylum. I hoped very much that things would settle, and I would be able to go back to Afghanistan upon completion of my master's degree. That first year that I lived in the UK (2006–2007) was enough to come to this understanding that asylum seekers, refugees, and migrants are not only unwelcome, they are also stigmatised. On the train to university, I could read the tabloids and see how the British media and the right-wing politicians particularly targeted asylum seekers who arrived irregularly and portrayed them as a threat to the general public.

Refugees were demonised and I did not want to be regarded as a threat.

That year studying at LSE for my master's degree was incredibly tough. I struggled to cope with the loneliness that had fallen upon me. The intensive one-year master programme tends to confine students to either the library or the small student residence room. I missed the ordinary sounds and smells of life. On top of this, I struggled with the course itself. I had changed my discipline and needed to work more to get familiar with the theories of sociology. I was also exposed to academic English for the first time, and this made me slower than my peers. Above all this, I was trying to come to terms with the reality that my relationship with my European partner was serious, but I could not see how I could tell my family and convince them to accept him as my husband. This emotional burden took a toll on me, and I started having mental health issues and had to seek medical support. At some point, I was so unwell that I was advised to quit my masters. But there was no way I could return to my parents as a failure. I had to bear the extreme anxiety, panic attacks, and nightmares of those days. I received extensions for my assignments and finally finished my degree.

After completion of my studies, I did return to Afghanistan but soon realised that the situation had deteriorated, and I could not stay. My UK visa was still valid and that allowed me to return to Europe. I decided to apply for the 'highly skilled migrant programme' that would give me two more years to stay in the UK and time to look for a job. My plan was to find a job and stay in the UK for two more years and observe the circumstances in

Afghanistan from a distance and decide whether it could be safe for me to return. I was confident that my work experience in a so-called developing 'post-conflict' country and a degree from a prestigious university would help me to get a job quickly. I had learnt that asylum seekers are regarded as non-Western and non-white people who are after the social benefits of the UK and are an economic burden. I did not want to be regarded as a burden. I was educated and I knew I could work and be independent the way I used to work and be financially independent in Afghanistan. If I could extend my visa via the 'highly skilled migrant programme', I would be considered as an asset to their economy and not as a burden.

I stayed with a Hazara family that I got to know during my studies in London. I shared a room with their toddler daughter who was learning, with difficulty, to sleep on her own. I had found an informal job in a Hazara business in southwest London. The distance from my accommodation in northeast London and the informal job was quite long and it took around two hours to get there. I was overqualified and underpaid for the job, and my boss' treatment was not appropriate, but I needed the salary to pay for my living costs, mostly for the visa application costs and food. I did not have to pay rent and my friend let me eat with them if needed. It was not an ideal situation, and I was clearly a burden. I hoped to be able to find a formal and well-paid job. I had managed to save a few hundred pounds but had to spend them for a critical health issue in a private clinic as I had no access to the NHS. I was broke and time was running out and I was getting very anxious that I would overstay my UK visa.

Despite meeting all the requirements to prove that I am a skilled migrant, my visa application was rejected. One of the reasons was the lack of evidence. I did not have a birth certificate, although copies of my valid Afghan passport with valid UK visa were attached to the application. I did not have a birth certificate because I was born at home, in a remote industrial dairy farm located in an impoverished suburb of Tehran. My parents registered me as their child without the need to present a certificate. I was registered as a refugee from birth and lived with that status until we were forced to go to Afghanistan in 2004. Moreover, the closest town with a hospital must have been hours away by car. But my family had just arrived from Afghanistan in the late 1970s and could not afford to spend their hard-earned and small salary for hospital appointments. I was my mother's second child, she had already given birth to one at home in Daykundi. I was left with no option but to claim asylum in the UK. I went to the Home Office in Croydon, south London, and started the process.

Afghanistan embassy

My Afghan passport says I was born in Daykundi, central Afghanistan. But I have never seen central Afghanistan and as I mentioned above, I missed my first and last opportunity to visit it with my parents. Upon our involuntary repatriation to Afghanistan from Iran in 2004, I applied for a *Tazkira* (national identification document) based on the records of my father in the ministry of internal affairs. He was born in Daykundi, and if I wanted to have a *Tazkira*, the place of my birth could only be

Daykundi. I demanded the Afghan authorities write 'Tehran' as my place of birth, but I was mocked by them. To obtain a *Tazkira* or any documents proving our identity as citizens of Afghanistan has always been a struggle for Iran-born and Iran-raised returnees. This struggle is extended to Afghan government representatives abroad.

The need to visit the embassy of Afghanistan has always made me feel uncomfortable. No matter if it is in Iran or here in the West, I have always been made conscious of my racialised, gendered, and minoritized status in Afghanistan. What has made my position more vulnerable was my Iranian-accented Farsi, which despite my efforts, has always betrayed me and signalled the fact that I have lived in Iran. I needed a birth certificate for the 'highly skilled migrant programme' that would allow me to extend my stay in the UK. I hoped the Embassy of Afghanistan would help me with a letter explaining the situation, but they were not willing to help.

During my life so far, I have only spent two consecutive years in Afghanistan (2004–2006), one year from mid-2015 to mid-2016 to conduct ethnographic research, two-week trips in 2017 and 2018 to introduce my son to my family, and a week in May 2021 to hold a funeral ceremony for my father. The rest of my life I have spent in Iran (25 years) and then here in the UK (16 years). Even though I have not lived in Afghanistan long and I myself feel so uncomfortable in the embassy of that country, it is so ironic that I am only recognised as a person from Afghanistan.

The stigmatising, criminalisation, and humiliation of applying for asylum

What I was experiencing as an asylum seeker in the UK was the result of tightening immigration policies introduced by the 'Immigration, Asylum and Nationality Act 2006'. This act gave the immigration authorities the right to obtain my biometric data, apparently for the purpose of proving I am the rightful holder of my passport. Asylum seekers, by fault, were considered dishonest, and therefore, the contrary should be proved.

In order to claim asylum, I had gone to the Home Office in Croydon. At that time, one could turn up at the Home Office and there was no need for a prior appointment. I arrived early in the morning and faced a long queue. We went through a tight security check and then entered the buildings. The first appointment was for screening when the date for the second appointment is determined. In the screening interview, my interviewer was a black lady who asked me general questions about my details and then briefly asked about the reason I claimed asylum. I remember that I was asked to provide the birth date of my grandparents, parents, and siblings, and I could not remember all and did not know some of them. My parents did not know their own birthdate and had to invent a date based on the rough data they had, but they had recorded their children's birthday. Celebrating birthdays was not common in our family until older siblings started celebrating for the younger ones. The interviewer expressed surprise and scepticism. I was also asked whether I am affiliated to any terrorist organisations or have committed any acts of terrorism. I remembered I was asked similar questions when I applied for the British visa in 2006. We are by default prone to being terrorists and must acknowledge in advance if we are not. These assumptions hurt.

In the second interview, I told the full story. I gave full details of how my relationship with my colleague had caused tension in my work and later in my immediate family. I also explained that I decided to return to the UK as I was confident I could apply for the 'Highly Skilled Migrant Programme' and stay two years longer and this time was enough to look for a job. According to the British immigration law, a person who flees for his/her life should claim asylum as soon as s/he enters the land of Britain. I did not claim asylum as soon as I returned to London. I was therefore charged with the offence of deceiving the immigration officer verbally at the airport as I did not reveal that I would like to claim for asylum. It was not my intention to claim asylum when I re-entered the UK, but the interviewer did not want to believe me. I was not aware of such rules. The immigration laws and rules keep changing, and it is not reasonable to expect people who flee for their lives to know European languages and keep them-selves updated with the latest changes in the immigration laws of the countries they go to. Many asylum seekers who take the land route and travel irregularly have no clue which country they will end up in.

The interviewer in the second interview was also a black lady and she recorded my voice this time. I felt betrayed that a woman of colour is charging another woman of colour with an offence, not knowing how people of colour reproduce white supremacy and unjust structures by behaving 'white'. One should not be surprised to see the brown women Priti Patel and Suella Braverman amongst the most hostile UK Home Secretaries to migrants and refugees. And while I write this piece, Rishi Sunak, the first brown Prime Minister of the UK vows to deport asylum seekers who come to the UK by boat to Rwanda.

When I was informed that I had been charged, I was quite confused. I was not sure if I had understood correctly and doubted my English. I remained quiet and composed. The reality hit me when I was taken into a room and someone started taking pictures of me, very much like the thriller movies in which a criminal is caught and photographed from various angles. When they took pictures of my profiles, both to the right and to the left, I started suspecting that something was going wrong. My biometrics were taken for the first time in my life. I waited in a room for a long time, then I was directed towards a car. As soon as I got out, I was shocked to see the van. It looked like the fenced police cars used for transporting prisoners. Something broke in me. I sat in the car with a few other young women. We did not exchange any words. The drive felt so long. The long winter nights had set in and I could not see where we were going. I wept quietly until we arrived in the Yarl's Wood Immigration Removal Centre. I had been put on a fast-track route where people are more likely to be rejected and sent back to their 'country of origin'.

Performing asylum

Asylum seekers and refugees learn about the constructed images of them in the west and try to behave the way they are expected to in order to maximise their chance of an asylum grant. My friend from Sierra Leone knew that she needed to prove whatever 'story' she presented. She had several significant and pressing reasons that would qualify her for an asylum grant, but she decided to only present the ones that the immigration officers would be most likely to believe or are trained to consider as valid cases. This case was very similar to an Afghan undocumented young man whom I had met in London later. He had claimed asylum as a minor in the UK and had to go through an ordeal until he was finally rejected. He was victim of sexual violence but was too ashamed to use as his case for asylum, but rather relied on persecution by the Taliban to present his case.

I found the whole experience of claiming asylum humiliating. Most of the staff in the prison felt entitled to maltreat the inmates in a patronising and infantilizing manner. I decided to limit my interaction with the staff to avoid further humiliation and instead spent time in the library. It was a very quiet library as most of the books were in English and most of the inmates were not fluent in English. There, I found an interesting shelf on which there were thick folders titled 'country profile'. I took down the 'Afghanistan Country Profile' in which there was general information on Afghanistan and the grounds on which one could grant asylum to a person from Afghanistan. I found it was like a 'cheat sheet' based on which I could frame my answers in my asylum interview. I was fluent in English, and I could read and learn from it, but this was not the case for most of my mates in the prison. In my original 'story', I wanted to explain that my life in Afghanistan is in danger because my colleagues disapproved of my behaviour and started sending me threatening emails. The corrupt Afghan police who hold traditional beliefs would not have been able or willing to protect me. But after reading the 'Afghanistan Country Profile', I realised that I must also highlight my ethnicity and religion as well as my gender to increase my chance of acceptance. This would have not occurred to me had I not read this report.

Grant of asylum

A few days after I arrived in the prison, I was given an interview date. I was extremely anxious as data showed that the interview was simply to meet the formalities and I would eventually be deported. While I was waiting for my interview, I was given leaflets on voluntary return and the financial support that comes with it. These made me more anxious.

A white lady interviewed me for my asylum application in the prison. A female Iranian interpreter had come with her, but as I was fluent in English and not happy with the translation, we decided to continue the interview without an interpreter. The interpreter was unfamiliar with the context of Afghanistan and the situation of refugees from Afghanistan in Iran. The interpreter expressed surprise, in Farsi, when I gave my accounts of racism towards refugees in Iran. I found her uncomfortable when I talked about Iran and the mistreatment by the Iranian government and public of the refugees. There were details that the interpreter was not able to transmit to the interviewer due to her ignorance.

In addition, the asylum application interviewers have a reputation for being strict and trying hard to find faults in your case or 'pull up a string of hair from yoghurt' to use a Persian proverb. My partner had access to the Internet and could help me find and compile evidence for my case. He wrote a statement and managed to get a statement from the head of the NGO I worked with. The interview was long, and we had to have a break in time. There I saw my legal advisor for the second time. Being in a prison was upsetting in itself and recalling what has happened to me in detail had made me more upset. Above all, knowing your life and future depends on this interview and the judgement of the interviewer create an immense amount of psychological pressure. I recalled what I had remembered from my life in Afghanistan and what could serve my case, but to my surprise, I had to make a lot of effort to explain why I should not be deported to Iran, my birthplace, but which would not accept responsibility for a non-citizen.

I waited around a week until the result of my interview came. I had a meeting with the interviewer, and she gave me the news and wished me well. I was among the rarest cases who could leave that prison with a grant of asylum. I think it was simply because I was fluent in English and that had made access to resources easier. I also had someone equally fluent in English outside the prison who was resourceful and could help me with finding evidence. My roommate had very limited knowledge of English and relatives back in Sudan who could not afford to invest the same resources in her application. I see why the rate of grant applications was very low in that prison. As I was now legally a refugee with status, I was immediately removed from the prison. I received the news of my application in the afternoon and by night, I was in a car towards an emergency accommodation. I arrived at the centre at night and left it at night. I have no memory of how that centre looks from outside and never wished to know. I decided to put the humiliating memory of this centre in the very back of my mind. I had no sense of where this emergency accommodation was located, but I remember I stayed in a church that had been transformed into an emergency accommodation. I stayed in a few more places until I was given a place in a hostel to wait for social housing.

After asylum

The hostel was located in Goldhawk road, west London, and close to Shepherd's Bush. The hostel was for single people or people not accompanied by their families and predominantly occupied by asylum seekers from Eritrea. An Iranian man and I were the only Farsi speakers. We were all given one bedroom each. Toilets and bathrooms and kitchen were all shared. We were not allowed to have visitors overnight and no children were allowed. Compared with my life as a student, the life in that hostel was closer to the life I was used to. Gradually, I made friends with some women from Eritrea, one of whom later became my son's godmother. While I was living in this hostel, I found my first job as a Human Rights Officer in a health charity. Contrary to the British public and state perception, most of us in the hostel wanted to put the trauma we experienced behind us and build a new life in the UK, find jobs, and start paying taxes.

After this job, I decided to pursue my PhD in Geneva in 2011. My refugee status complicated my situation. As a refugee in the UK, I was not allowed to be out of the UK for more than three months at a time but studying for my PhD required at least one year and half to be based in Geneva. I made sure to go back to the UK every three months. The restriction on my mobility also meant I changed my research proposals and field research and conducted it instead in the UK among refugees from Afghanistan. Meantime, I had started the time-consuming and painstaking task of negotiating my marriage with my family. My status had changed and so too my bargaining power with my family. I was financially independent and contributed financially to family costs in Afghanistan.

Once I was granted asylum, I was also given a refugee or 'Convention' travel document with which I was able to travel to some countries. This travel document was for stateless people and with it I could not be fully Afghan or British. Despite holding a travel document, whose main purpose is to facilitate travelling, I was always nervous approaching the British border police who always found some reason to pick on me. My partner, being a white Western middle-class man, had the privilege of freely travelling around the world for work and pleasure and I accompanied him sometimes, wherever my travel document was recognised. I was the one constantly cornered and questioned at the border and sarcastically called 'a very well-travelled young lady'.

After the grant of asylum, I needed to wait for five years to be granted indefinite leave to remain. The time I spent in the UK before my asylum application, which was nearly two years as a student, would not be counted. In 2013, I was eligible to apply for indefinite leave to remain. It took one year for my application to be processed, and during this time, I was confined in the UK with no travel document. The application for 'naturalisation' is the next step after obtaining a permanent visa in the UK, and this was supposed to be a smooth process. However, I had to wait another year or so to be eligible for naturalisation. After obtaining my indefinite leave to remain, I was kept waiting for a long time without any information on why my naturalisation application takes so much time. With the recommendation of a friend, I decided to seek legal help and it was not cheap. My lawyer managed to obtain information from the Home Office system through 'The Freedom of Information Act' in which it was stated that as I had deceived the immigration officer verbally, there was doubt whether I am eligible to be a British citizen. The Home Office never told me why they were delaying, otherwise I would have tried to 'prove' I am a good person and 'worthy' of being a citizen. My lawyer asked me to bring evidence that I am a good person! I compiled a few documents and one of them was a letter of recommendation from my PhD supervisor. In his letter, he stressed that I am an academic person and will contribute to British academia and that he knows me personally and has full trust in me. I had also attached my CV in which it showed that I started working a few months after being granted asylum and paid tax in this country. I also attached letters from my pro-fessional manager. These were sent to the Home Office via my lawyer, and it worked. In June 2015, I finally received my British passport. The first country I travelled to was Afghanistan in July 2015. It was to conduct ethnographic research in Mazar-e Sharif, the city where my family lived. I embarked on a research project and could spend an unforgettable year with my family after a very long time. In the same year, I officially got married with my partner and received my parent's blessings. The discrimination that had forced me to leave Afghanistan in 2006 had not ended. The situation has deteriorated, especially with regard to security. This year was different from 2004 to 2006 because I had entered

Afghanistan as a British citizen and employed by a Western university. My legal and social status had changed and that hugely impacted my stay in the country.

Despite all the challenges mentioned above, I have built a life in the UK. And that was mainly possible because I was among the lucky few who are legally recognised. For any asylum seeker, legal recognition is the most important step towards building a life in a given country. To be a 'citizen' with legally recognised equal access to resources and opportunities was something I felt first in the UK. Had I been given the possibility of having legal recognition in Iran, my birth country, I would have taken a different path in my life. Had I been given equal opportunities as a 'returnee' Hazara Shia woman in Afghanistan, I would have also taken a different path in my life. Lack of legal recognition in Iran and racism, prejudice, discrimination, and the violence that it induced in Afghanistan was the impulse for my family, relatives, and all the Hazaras in our community to migrate to further and riskier destinations to improve their lives.

Transnational families

My family members now are torn apart and scattered in different countries. Similar to any typical family from Afghanistan, we practice a form of 'cosmopolitanism from below' or a kind of 'forced cosmopolitanism'. The protracted conflict in Afghanistan has caused several waves of exoduses and people have settled in various locations around the world. Afghans, therefore, build their social networks across several nation-states and in this transnational social space various dynamics are nurtured. I have siblings in Iran, Kazakhstan, Germany, Denmark, the UK, and Australia.

My father's eternal resting place happened to be in Iran and my mother's on a hill in Kazakhstan. My parents' premature deaths were caused by their marginalised status as refugees in Iran and Kazakhstan. Both lost their lives in 2021 to Covid-19 while waiting at the end of the queue for vaccination. My first cousins and other extended family members are all scattered out across the globe, mostly in Europe. Having been raised in a community-centred society, the imposed separations from people we grew up with and love weighs on our hearts. However, new technologies facilitate this transnationalism and make communication easier and more frequent.

Despite being transnational, the Hazaras in particular and Afghans in general are not a homogenous community in the countries in which they have settled. Afghans have left Afghanistan in various waves in response to different triggers, whether political upheavals, conflict, drought, or economic hardship. The last most recent wave of migration out of Afghanistan was triggered by the Taliban's takeover of the country in 2021. Hundreds of thousands of Afghans were evacuated (including my co-authors Abdullah and Reza) and many left and continue to leave the country after the chaotic departure of the 'international community' or US-led NATO forces in Afghanistan. My sister and her family were evacuated to Australia and my elder brother and his family to Germany at that time. That experience has forged a bond among those forced to leave so abruptly. However, in spite of that common traumatic experience, Afghan communities in the diaspora are still divided along ethnic, linguistic, religious, and political grounds.

'Still water stagnates, one must not stay still'

Around mid-June 2024, I had dropped my son to school and had few child-free hours. I decided to go to the hairdressing salon in our neighbourhood, which is run by some women of Turkish origin. I live in Edmonton Green, northeast London, where a large community of Turkish people live. It is a very lively, dynamic and yet deprived and working-class neighbourhood. I wanted to have my hair trimmed as the wedding of a Hazara friend with an English man was approaching. One of the good things about this hair salon was the fact that one did not need to have a prior appointment and could appear any time. As my schedule as a working mother with a child with special needs is constantly changing, this is perfect for me. I went inside and as soon as I saw Elif, I was pleased. Unintentionally, I had become her regular client and she had become my trusted hairdresser. Elif came to me smiling and asked me to wait for a while until she finished with another client. I grabbed a chair and while sitting, I noticed that one of the hairdressers was talking to two of her customers in Farsi. She was telling her client in Farsi that she had requested her Turkish colleagues not to disclose the fact that she speaks Farsi. It was because she does not want anyone to understand that she is Iranian. I interrupted to let her know that I speak Farsi and I understood what she was saying. I wanted to be ethical, so to speak, as I thought they may disclose some private information. The three of them turned their heads in surprise and asked with half-smiling faces, 'are you Iranian?' I said to myself, what a complicated question! I said I was born in Iran and spent most of my life there, but my parents are from central Afghanistan. The Iranian customer cut me off with a righteous look and said, 'So you are an *Afghani*'. I replied that I had only lived three years in Afghanistan. I was thinking how to explain here in this hair salon in simple language the citizenship debates that I used to have in tutorials with my university students. The words remained in my mouth when she said again 'If your parents are *Afghani*, then you are *Afghani*'. I repeated 'I lived in Afghanistan for only three years of my whole life'. She said 'No, you are *Afghani*'. Every time she uttered the word *Afghani*, I felt a slap on my face. Then, the three of them continue in Farsi between themselves. The lady responsible for eyebrow threading came to me and asked if my eyebrows needed threading. I said why not! Once my eyebrows were done, Elif came and looked after my hair. While she was carefully working on my hair, I went into my bubble and wondered how this term *Afghani* still had the power to hurt me.

In writing this chapter and reflecting on my experience of claiming asylum in the UK, I am conscious that I have made myself vulnerable by sharing experiences that I did not dare to share with my own family in Afghanistan. It has become comfortable to share after realising that the Hazaras who have been born or raised in Iran have experienced similar multiple layers of racialisation, discrimination, and humiliation while on the move. We rationalised our trajectory by holding on to this common belief that 'Still water stagnates, one must not stay still'. We are *Awarah* (wanderers) and the status of *Awaragi* (wandering) defines who we are. My trajectory is not unique, and the contributors of this book share much of it. This chapter has demonstrated how my trajectory can be located in a broader phenomenon: I built a life in the UK. I have a home and a small family. I am highly educated and have a career. But the scar of this experience remains on my soul. In other words, the migration experience generally and the asylum system in particular humiliated me and kept telling me that I am small, that I am unimportant, and I should do what I am told, and that I have no value. In spite of those, I struggle but I continue. I have made friendships and networks, and there is solidarity but there is a constant battle, and we bear the scar of this battle.

6
Lessons learnt

The previous chapters told individual and collective stories of migration. In this chapter, we draw together the knowledge and experiences contained in these stories to illustrate and challenge some of the theories that have evolved to explain different aspects of forced migration. The chapter is divided into five different sections, each of which has at least one learning objective embedded.

In the first, we look at how our experiences have been shaped by social structures, including laws and policies, as well as conflict, economics, and history. But our stories have also shown that migrants are not just passive victims of these structures—each chapter of this book chronicles the choices that we and our communities have made as we have negotiated, challenged, been defeated by, or overcome these structures.

The second section interrogates the different categories into which migrants are forced and explores the value and limitations of categories. Reflecting on the preceding chapters, we highlight the ways in which we have all migrated across the boundaries between economic migrant, labour migrant, refugee, student, highly skilled migrant, and undocumented migrant.

Although there is some literature on the link between migration and racism, work on racism as a driver of migration and as a response to migration is still limited, so we address this in the third section. The experiences of the authors here demonstrate how racism has been interwoven into every stage of our lives and how each different experience of forced migration exposed us to a new variation of hostility, whether based on our physical being, our perceived religion, our accent and culture, or our migration status.

Policy is largely shaped by the three accepted durable solutions in relation to forced migrants: return, resettlement, or integration into the host community, and these describe the outcomes for many people but do not represent a solution for all forced migrants or only following prolonged periods where none apply. The fourth section explores some of the problematic assumptions underpinning these solutions, as well as examining some alternative possibilities.

This book is part of a series on forced migration, and details the migrations forced upon all four of us. While inevitably, we did make choices and shaped our migration to an extent, it was definitely not freely or lightly chosen—it was often a reaction to negative events and forces. And yet, as this fifth section illustrates, we have made the best of our experiences.

Structure and agency

The previous chapters demonstrate the battle waged by each of us, by our communities, and by forced migrants all around the world as we try to survive and, as far as possible, to thrive and reach our potential in the face of structural barriers. By structural barriers, we mean political, economic, social factors in our countries of origin, exile, and transit. Political factors include policies, laws, ideologies, international relations, and of course, the existence of conflict. Economic factors include employment opportunities, wage differentials, and the costs of migrating. Social factors include culture: whether there is a culture of migration in society, whether migration is viewed negatively, is there a shared language or history, the degree of ethnic, religious, or gender equality or discrimination.

When our parents left Afghanistan, they fled conflict between warring groups, persecution because of their ethnicity or religion, and poverty that was due both to economic underdevelopment and discrimination. They were driven out by forces they could not control, structural forces. Peaceful, stable, wealthy countries that do not discriminate against sections of their populations do not produce large numbers of forced migrants. Afghans, by contrast, constitute one of the largest populations of forced migrants in the world (UNHCR, 2024).

And yet, not everyone left. It could be argued that there was an element of choice. Many Hazara stayed in Afghanistan even during the worst of times. All of us have family members in Afghanistan who did not want to leave or wanted to leave but could not. Some people did not even have the minimal resources necessary to travel to, or to cross, the border. People move but not in circumstances of their own choosing. We exercise agency, but that agency is shaped and limited by structural factors. And we in turn shape those factors, altering the culture, pooling resources, resisting policies.

While we were victims of global forces, we were not passive: we pooled resources to send individuals to safety. When visas were unattainable, like Abdullah we found guides to take us across borders; faced with limited access to education, Hazara in Iran and Pakistan set up their own schools or, like Atefeh, insisted painstakingly on her right to attend university in Iran. Our families supported us and provided us with the social capital necessary to overcome some, but not all, structural barriers, and as a result, our generation of Hazara exiles built social capital that permitted us greater mobility and safer routes than experienced by our parents.

Migration has long been a survival strategy for Afghans in times of crisis (Monsutti, 2005). When conflict or natural disasters made survival impossible, people moved to neighbouring areas until the crisis passed, and they could return and rebuild. When poverty or entrepreneurship pushed people to leave, they travelled across the Asian continent, buying and selling goods, working as labourers, studying, seeking opportunities that could not be found at home, returning when they could to families left behind (Hussaini et al., 2021). But structural factors also shaped where people went. In general, and especially when forced to flee as family groups, people seek out the nearest safe place so that they can return easily, because it is less expensive and because it is familiar.

Afghanistan's borders did not always exist: Iran and Afghanistan were once united and continue to share a common religion and language. The border between Afghanistan and Pakistan is relatively recent and, until recently, was easily crossed. Both countries host large Afghan diaspora that offer support and refuge in times of trouble, even in the face of hostility from host states. Though our accents and dialects set us apart, as previous chapters demonstrated, we can understand each other. This made surviving in exile possible, as there was work for us to do.

Like migrants everywhere, we served as a reserve army of labour, doing the jobs disdained by Iranian citizens, and for lower wages. States have welcomed us for political and economic reasons: generosity to us meant aid from the international community was controlled by the Pakistan government; our fathers, brothers, husbands, and sons were used to fight by the Iranian government or to fill labour shortages. The legal structures that excluded us from the citizenry, confined us to low skilled sectors of the labour market, limited our access to education, racialized us as inferior shaped our migration experiences in neighbouring countries, and taught us that we would never belong. But our communities were not content to remain labourers, carpet weavers, tailors, and porters. Forced to make a living in sweatshops and building sites, some of us are also poets and painters (Olszewska, 2015).

Our 'return' to the country of our citizenship, if not our birth, has also been shaped by our 'host' states, who have forced us, as in the case of Khadija and her family, to leave countries that we were not allowed to call home for a homeland that felt alien. In the following sections, we examine in greater detail the concepts of return and reintegration, and the serial racialization experienced by our communities.

The decision to seek safety and a new home in the Global North was forced on many of us. Hundreds of thousands of Hazara decided that since we could never be 2nd or even 3rd class citizens in Iran and Pakistan, and since there was no safety, employment, or equality in Afghanistan, we would have to travel beyond the neighbouring countries. We four have within our close family circles relatives who chose to defy those structures that limited their horizons and their mobility and risk their lives in the hope of finding somewhere that they could build a life and realise their potential. All were aware that they would have to overcome obstacles placed in their way by hostile states, but all believed that they had the necessary luck, determination and autonomy to make it to Europe or Australia. Fewer were aware that laws, policies, and state institutions would exact a price for the audacity of claiming the right to move, a price that in some cases included their lives (Abbasi, 2016).

The barriers put in place by states increase the cost and risk of these journeys. Increasingly, people who have no choice but to move, whether from home or a place of exile, are forced to use facilitators who may be honest brokers, as in the case of Abdullah's cousin, or brutal criminals. The increasing restrictions on mobility, especially from the Global South, have turned smuggling into a lucrative and global business. A clear illustration of the role of states in creating and maintaining this business was what followed Angela Merkl's response to the arrival of hundreds of thousands of Syrians fleeing civil war in 2015. When the German Chancellor announced 'Wir schaffen das' (we can manage this), borders in and around Europe opened. Afghans, fleeing escalating conflict and insecurity (see Chapter 1), were suddenly able to travel through Turkey and into Greece relatively easily. A journey that could take years and tens of thousands of euros could now be accomplished in 14 days for less than 1,000 euros without recourse to smugglers. When the borders slammed shut, and people found themselves stranded along border fences, batted back and forth between different border patrols, the smuggling business came back with a vengeance.

One consequence of the high price exacted for entry to the Global North is that return to one's community is made, if not impossible, then very difficult. Given that the only way for many Afghans to reach Europe is by investing months and years of one's life and the family's resources, and preserving the hopes and dreams of the family, giving up is not an option. We are forced to remain in states where we cannot feel at home (Schuster and Majidi, 2013, 2014).

Abdullah, Khadija, and Reza had travelled to Europe as students, as participants in conferences and workshops, but the final departure was not chosen but imposed. Our decision to leave, to give up on hopes and dreams of a future in Afghanistan, was in response to discrimination, persecution, and the threat of violence to us and our families, experiences common to many Afghans, especially Hazara Shia. However, unlike most of our community, we had the advantage of speaking English, of an education, of having contacts in the UK, Sweden, and elsewhere in Europe, and most importantly, we were not forced to travel overland or by sea without documents and without resources.

Compared with most of our community members, we were lucky, though it did not always feel that way.

The global north is not generally very welcoming to forced migrants and in recent decades has put filters in place in countries of origin. For example, European embassies in Kabul closed their consular divisions, so that when Afghans wished to apply for visas, we were obliged first to apply for an Iranian or Pakistani visa, travel to Tehran or Islamabad, and make our applications there. In Reza's case, he, his wife, and three children spent six weeks in a hotel room in Islamabad waiting for the British embassy there to decide whether or not to grant them a visa. Had they refused, the time and expense of that journey would have been stolen from them (Khosravi, 2018). Khadija too had to travel to Islamabad, missing the opportunity to visit her family home in Daykundi.

These restrictions move European borders far from European territories and ensure that access is reserved for those who can pay or who are prepared to risk their lives crossing mountains, seas, and militarised borders as undocumented migrants. As in the Global South, those without documents find themselves vulnerable to exploitation, forced to work cash in hand, for lower wages and without access to the social protections enjoyed by those in regular employment. Without documents, forced migrants are especially vulnerable to the threat of deportation and so hyper-exploitable (De Genova, 2002). This vulnerability is a product of state policies towards forced migrants.

Our stories demonstrate that, even when forced to move by real and imminent threats to security, we decide to move though not in circumstances of our choosing. This blurs the conceptual boundaries between voluntary and involuntary mobility (Bakewell, 2008; Hyndman, 2012; Monsutti, 2008).

Migrant categories

Undocumented migrant, economic migrant, labour migrant, refugee, student, highly skilled migrant—together we four have at different times occupied all of these categories and some of them simultaneously. Migration is a process with different, though blurred and overlapping, stages in which gender, legal categories, skills, networks all play a role. It is very difficult to untangle the different phenomena which make up our experiences and which are woven through the different chapters. In telling our stories, we have tried to convey the complexity of forced migration, a complexity that cannot be captured by simplistic or rigid categories. Acknowledging this complexity is vital in gaining an understanding of the myriad experiences of migrants around the world.

In this book, the importance of legal categories is clear. Such categories are constructed, predominantly by states, and imposed on those who move, largely for the convenience of receiving states. They are not 'natural' and are not a true reflection of how we migrants see ourselves. They exist to facilitate the decision-making of states and their representatives, and key to making those decisions easy and efficient is the erasure of our humanity. In the previous chapter, Khadija describes the humiliation and pain of trying to fit one category, highly skilled migrant, only to be stripped of everything but her status as a woman with a weak claim to asylum.

Since many states have acknowledged a particular obligation to admit those who are refugees, or close family members, but recognise no legal or moral obligation to admit anyone else, they have created definitions, or 'ideal types' to which real people only occasionally conform (such as the definition of a refugee contained in article 1 of the 1951 Geneva Convention relating to the status of refugees), and these serve to filter those who would enter. States have created particular kinds of gateways into their territories, and migrants are forced to try and fit into matching categories if they want to gain entry and/or residence, as Khadija found when trying to apply for asylum. However, many migrants move through these categories, crossing between 'legality' and 'illegality', switching from being refugees to students to workers, undocumented migrants to asylum seekers, temporary to permanent migrants and often fitting more than one category simultaneously. As Atefeh found, in order to become a university student in Iran, it was necessary to stop being a refugee, return to Afghanistan and apply for an Iranian student visa. These categories hide the fact that refugees need to work to support themselves and their families, students, or highly skilled migrants find that changes at home mean they are unable to return and must apply for asylum. However, as Khadija found, state officials find it difficult to accept that forced migrants can and do fit multiple categories simultaneously.

These categories are also normative implying, more or less explicitly, judgements about those to whom they are applied, and as such they reveal quite a lot about the person or institution doing the defining. For example, during the Cold War, refugees as defined by the 1951 Refugee Convention were seen in the West as 'good guys' – defenders of democracy, human rights, and freedoms. In the Soviet Union, conversely, they were seen as traitors. For the Soviet Union, refugees should have been more properly understood as those forced to flee poverty. Later, Afghan refugees in Pakistan were warriors resisting Soviet invaders, only to be classed as terrorists after 9/11. In Iran, we were welcomed as *Muhajir*, fleeing to protect our religion, but then reviled as criminals and drug addicts, as *Afghanis*, to be arrested and deported as undesirable.

Categories are important because different types of migrants are entitled to different bundles of rights and are received more or less positively, though these attitudes can change over time. 'Economic' or labour migrants may be regarded positively when they contribute to economic growth and reconstruction and fill obvious labour gaps, as we did in Iran in the 1980s. But much depends on the narrative constructed by host states. When Iran decided it no longer needed migrant labour, we were told we had a duty to return to Afghanistan, to rebuild our country. As described by Reza, many young Afghans, born in Iran, were persuaded by those campaigns and the hope of finding a home where they would not face discrimination.

An ongoing search for safety, the Russian doll of persecution

Hannah Arendt writing in response to the publication of the Universal Declaration of Human Rights (UDHR) in 1948, herself a stateless refugee having fled Nazi occupied Europe, noted that

those rights depended on belonging to a state that would protect them. Her assessment rings true for us:

> Something much more fundamental than freedom
> and justice, which are rights of citizens, is at stake when
> belonging to the community into which one is born
> is no longer a matter of course and not belonging no
> longer a matter of choice (Arendt 1986: 296)

Rejected by the country into which we were born/raised, Iran,
and the country of our citizenship, Afghanistan, we were forced
to throw ourselves on the mercy of states that, having under-
written the UDHR and the Refugee Convention, confined us in
camps while they decided whether or not our rights should be
respected.

Until recently, we have not had the protection of a state. Arendt
noted that when attacked as a Jew, one must defend oneself as a
Jew, not as a German or a bearer of human rights (1986. We four
have been attacked as Hazara, as Shia, as Afghans, as refugees
and forced migrants, and, in the case of Atefeh and Khadija, as
women. We are fighting on so many fronts. The social group to
which the four of us belong has experienced serial racialization,
and in escaping one form, we have inevitably found ourselves
subjected to another.

When we speak of racialization, we mean a 'continuous process of
positioning and identity construction', a process that puts people
into categories that are not fixed or natural (Phoenix, 2005), but
where meaning is attached to particular, often physical but also
cultural and legal, characteristics, and where these categories
are used to justify treating people unequally. In Afghanistan, we

have been racialized as Hazara because of our physical appearance, which means that we are presumed to be Shia, presumed to be fit only for low skilled work. A similar process occurs in Iran, but there our physical appearance means we are racialized as *Afghani*, whereas those Afghans who are not physically different are able to pass, to integrate. In a Shia society, our religion is not relevant, as it is in Afghanistan. Our legal status is important, but often less important than our identity as *Afghani*, meaning that we can be arrested, detained, and deported despite papers that proclaim our right to be present. To return to Arendt (1986, 296), in a society in which we are excluded from the political community, where we do not have the right to have rights (the case in Afghanistan and Iran), we are excluded even from the possibility of fighting for our freedom and all that is left to us is slavery or flight.

Fanon defined racialization as the process through which differences between Africans are erased by the category of 'negro', a process for which Europeans and colonists are responsible (1967). In Iran and in Europe, our Hazara and Shia identities were subsumed by that of *Afghani*, Afghan, migrant, or refugee. While Khadija found solidarity in the detention centre with other refugee women from Sudan and Sierra Leone (categorised as asylum seekers, they were refugees but without the resources to justify their claims), Reza, volunteering with evacuated Afghans found the different treatment of Ukrainian refugees impossible to explain without recourse to concepts of race and racism. Aside from phenotypic differences, it was clear that these white Christians were racialized as European, while Afghans were racialized as Muslim others.

Though posed to everyone applying for a visa, the nonsensical question as to whether we were affiliated to a terrorist organisation (what visa applicant would respond in the affirmative?) lands brutally with those of us who have fled the Taliban, contributes the humiliation imposed by a system that strips us of every identity, and forces us to adopt the sole position of victim. Khadija's chapter illustrates the impotence and fear generated by an asylum system underpinned by a culture of disbelief (Jubany, 2017). From a situation in which we are categorised by and reduced to, our ethnicity and religion, we are thrown into one in which we have no identity but that of an asylum seeker, to which only negative meaning is attributed.

Khadija and Atefeh both spoke of the restrictions placed on them by their gender. Even before the Taliban returned to power in 2021, patriarchal norms shaped the lives of Afghan women. On arrival in Afghanistan, Khadija's gendered identity intersected with her 'returnee' status, marital status, ethnicity, religion, and socio-economic status, and it shaped and influenced her experience of homecoming in Afghanistan where she felt rejected by the country she hoped to make a 'homeland'. Similarly, Atefeh's experience illustrated the obstacles she faced in pursuing her passion for studying cinematography as a refugee woman. Her refugee status, compounded by gender discrimination, made her even more vulnerable to systemic and arbitrary barriers. However, it is important to acknowledge how gender expectations also shaped the lives of men. In Iran, refugee men are expected to enter the job market at earlier ages and are therefore exposed to discrimination and deportation, and girls are more likely to get higher education. In Afghanistan, families invest in younger men to migrate to Europe through the dangerous land route and women stay home and pick up new roles and responsibilities.

The Hazara diaspora is growing, and it is conceivable that soon, if not already, it will outnumber those who remain in our traditional homeland. Increasingly, the new generation of Hazara, especially those outside Afghanistan, is insisting on foregrounding our Hazara identity. The extent to which this will remain a diasporic identity, forever associated with forced migration is unclear. We have already seen our population in Afghanistan massively reduced—and given the current regime, it seems unlikely that Hazara or Shia will feel safe in Afghanistan for a long time to come.

Finding a home? Return/repatriation, reintegration, or resettlement

The preferred durable solutions for forced migrants are return and reintegration in the country of origin, local integration in the country of first asylum, or resettlement to a third country when that is not possible. Integration is the expected outcome of each of these solutions, understood as equal access to the resources of citizens—whether in Afghanistan, neighbouring countries or countries of resettlement. This group of authors have between us experienced each of these 'solutions', without any of them being an unqualified success.

Local integration should be a means to allow forced migrants to end their exile in countries of first asylum and become full members of their host society, that is, citizens with the right to have rights. And yet, there are few successful examples of local integration. Most often, it is actively discouraged in countries of first asylum and Atefeh's chapter details the exclusion experienced by Afghans, and in particular Hazara, in Iran. Even when we were welcomed to Iran in the 1980s and allowed to integrate economically and socially, we were excluded politically. For many Hazara, we managed a degree of de facto integration, finding work, renting homes, enlisting the assistance of Iranians to buy those things forbidden to us: sim cards, motor bikes, shops. But without citizenship, our integration was contingent on our usefulness, and we remained confined to particular sectors of the menial labour market, excluded from education, and vulnerable to discrimination, abuse, and forced repatriation.

Voluntary repatriation was in principle the preferred solution to the refugee problem, considered in the best interest of the refugee, and a way of restoring social order to the state that had been disrupted by conflict (Chimni, 2000; Hammond, 1999), but in practice it was rarely possible. From the 1990s, the emphasis continued to be on return, but increasingly from the 1990s onwards states emphasised forced rather than voluntary return (Chimni, 2004), and reintegration was seen as a means to anchor people in their country of origin so that they would not try to leave again. While Reza's 'return' to Afghanistan was voluntary, Khadija and her family were expelled from Iran to Afghanistan. There is an extensive body of poetry by Afghans, even those born elsewhere, that voices the longing experienced by generations of Afghans to return 'home' to a place where they are known, where there is a shared understanding, a shared language, familiarity (Alavi Jafari and Schuster, 2019), but as Reza and Khadija show, this longing is often unsatisfied by the experience of 'return', leading to re-migration. However, (re)integration is not the inevitable result of return, especially when that return is forced, and when reintegration and assisted voluntary return programmes are little more than fig leaves to justify forced returns (Blitz et al., 2005; Van Houte et al., 2016). Perhaps more importantly, reintegration is not possible when the violence and discrimination that drove us out in the first place remains unchanged, or as is the case currently, is worse.

Given that neither 'return' nor local integration are realistic solutions, resettlement becomes a solution for a lucky few. The US, Canada and Australia have resettled forced migrants for decades. Resettlement allows states to screen candidates, to exclude those who would be a burden or a threat, to select those who will be a testament to their generosity, their liberalness, and progressiveness (Schuster, 2004). And for many, resettlement is the gateway to a settled future, one in which our children will have security and a life without violence, though not necessarily without racism.

Migration offers opportunities, but at what cost?

For we four, born/raised in exile in Iran, it is hard to be rejected by our country of birth. Once we leave, we can only ever return to Iran as tourists, and when we return we are not the same people who left. We now have experiences that those left behind do not share and that sets us apart. Though we miss all that was familiar, we do not want to return to a place in which we are not accepted and not treated as equals. We have been forced to leave our birthplaces and the home of our imagination, and now we are trying to make a new home, where we belong. The identity of our generation cannot be defined by a geographical location. More than place, it is our experience that defines our identity; the shared experience of being on the move, of not belonging to a specific place, of being rejected and of having a common trajectory.

As described by Monsutti (2005), we Hazara have always been embedded in transnational social networks, crossing and recrossing borders, creating a transnational space that in turn shapes our lives. In a way, this transnational space has become our homeland, the place where we recognise each other's suffering (Abbasi, 2019).

Perhaps we will always feel foreign in Europe or North America, perhaps we will never be completely at home, but our children will have the citizenship of countries in which ambitions to be world class scientists, entrepreneurs, or even prime minister are not impossible dreams.

Recommended projects

1. Make a list of ideas or questions you had when you started reading this book that have been answered, challenged, confirmed or raised by the stories here. Were there surprises? If so, what were they? What have you learned from the book that you would like others to know?

2. Trace your family's migration history—interview your parents, grandparents and extended family about their migration experiences, ask them about their decision-making, their journeys and their experiences of settling or not into a new society—compare and contrast those experiences with those of Abdullah, Atefe, Khadija and Reza.

3. Identify the main migrant communities where you live. Using desk-based research, investigate the history of one community's arrival in your home country—when did they arrive, what caused them to leave their homes, what brought them to yours? What has been the response of the government? Reflect on what this research has taught you. Did it reveal assumptions of which you were unaware.

4. If you were to design a new migration policy for your home country, what would it look like?

Notes

1. All proper names in the book are pseudonyms

2. According to Article 976 of the Civil Code of Iran, Iranian citizenship is granted to the following individuals:

    All individuals residing in Iran, except those with foreign citizenship.

    Anyone born to an Iranian father, whether in Iran or outside of Iran.

    Anyone born in Iran to parents of unknown nationality.

    Anyone born in Iran to foreign parents, provided one of the parents was born in Iran.

    Anyone born in Iran to a foreign father who arrived and has resided legally in Iran for at least one year after reaching the age of 18.

    Any foreign woman who marries an Iranian man.

    Any foreign national who has acquired Iranian citizenship.

3. The Roshanaee Movement, led by members of the Hazara community, emerged in Afghanistan in 2016 as a social and political campaign for justice, equality, and an end to discrimination. It began as a response to the Afghan government's decision to reroute a major power transmission line intended to bring electricity from Turkmenistan. Originally planned to pass through Bamiyan, a predominantly Hazara-populated and underdeveloped province, the route was changed to Salang Pass, bypassing Bamiyan. On July 23, 2016, a peaceful protest in Deh Mazang Square, Kabul, was targeted by a devastating ISIS-claimed suicide bombing. The attack killed at least 85 people and injured over 400, marking one of Kabul's deadliest incidents. The government's response was widely criticized as indifferent and incompetent.

References

Abbasi, K. (2016). 'Migration at any Cost'. Becomingadult.net. Available at: https://becomingadult.net/2016/02/01/migration-at-any-cost/ [Accessed 11 Dec. 2024].

Abbasi, K. (2019). 'There is death in immobility': An auto-ethnography of the identification process of transnational young Hazaras. PhD. Geneva, Graduate Institute of International and Development Studies.

Abbasi-Shavazi, M. J., Glazebrook, D., Jamshidiha, G., Mahmoudian, H. and Sadeghi, R. (2008). *Second-generation Afghans in Iran: Integration, Identity and Return*, Afghanistan Research and Evaluation Unit (AREU), April 2008, https://www.refworld.org/reference/countryrep/areu/2008/en/58734 [Accessed 27 Nov. 2024].

Adelkhah, F. and Olszewska, Z. (2007). The Iranian Afghans. *Iranian Studies*, 40(2), pp. 137–165. http://www.jstor.org/stable/4311887

Afghanistan Justice Report. (2005). Casting Shadows: War Crimes and Crimes against Humanity: 1978–2001, *Refworld* https://www.refworld.org/reference/countryrep/osi/2005/en/77878 [Accessed 22 Nov. 2024].

Ahmad, L. (n.d.). Sexual Violence: Unacceptable on All Counts. *Forced Migration Review*, Available at https://www.fmreview.org/ahmad/ [Accessed 22 Nov. 2024].

Ahmadi Dovlat, A. (2021). *Golshahr: Memories of a Geologist*. London: Nebesht Press.

Alavi Jafari, B. and Schuster, L. (2019). Representations of exile in Afghan Oral Poetry and Songs. *Crossings Journal of Migration and Culture*, 10(2), pp. 183–203. DOI:10.1386/cjmc_00002_1

Amir, A. (2019, 24 Nov). Golshahr [Music video]. YouTube. https://www.youtube.com/watch?v=AljWFLIuOrl

Aranda, E. M. (2007). *Emotional Bridges to Puerto Rico: Migration, Return Migration and the Struggles of Incorporation.* New York: Rowman and Littlefield.

Arendt, H. (1986). *The Origins of Totalitarianism.* London: Andre Deutsch.

Bakewell, O. (2008). Research Beyond the Categories: The Importance of Policy Irrelevant Research into Forced Migration. *Journal of Refugee Studies*, 21(4), pp. 432–453. https://doi.org/10.1093/jrs/fen042

Bleuer, C. (2012). State-Building, Migration and Economic Development on the Frontiers of Northern Afghanistan and Southern Tajikistan. *Journal of Eurasian Studies*, 3(1), pp. 69–79. https://doi.org/10.1016/j.euras.2011.10.008

Blitz, B. K., Sales, R. and Marzano, L. (2005). Non-Voluntary Return? The Politics of Return to Afghanistan. *Political Studies*, 53(1), pp. 182–200.

Chimni, B. S. (2004). From Resettlement to Involuntary Repatriation: Towards a Critical History of Durable Solutions to Refugee Problems. *Refugee Survey Quarterly*, 23(3), pp. 55–73.

Chimni, B. S. (2000). Globalization, Humanitarianism and the Erosion of Refugee Protection. *Journal of Refugee Studies*, 13(3), pp. 243–263.

Cohen, R. (2002). Afghanistan and the challenges of humanitarian action in time of war. *Forced Migration Review*, 13, pp. 23–27.

De Genova, N. P. (2002). Migrant 'illegality' and Deportability in Everyday Life. *Annual Review of Anthropology*, 31(1), pp. 419–447.

Fanon, F. (1967). *Black Skin, White Masks*. New York: Grove Press.

Hakimi, M. J. (2023). The Genocide of Hazaras. *Virginia Journal of International Law Online*, 63, pp. 21–32. Available at https://www.vjil.org/the-genocide-of-the-hazaras [Accessed 13 Dec. 2024].

Hammond, L. (1999). Examining the Discourse of Repatriation: Towards a More Proactive Theory of Return Migration. *The End of the Refugee Cycle*, pp. 227–244.

Hussaini, R., Hossaini, M., Rezaie, R., Schuster, L. and Shinwari, M. R. K. (2021). 'My beloved will come today or tomorrow' time and the left behind. In: M. Bhatia and V. Canning, eds., *Stealing Time: Migration, Temporalities and State Violence*. Cham, Switzerland: Springer International Publishing.

Hussaini, R. and Schuster, L. (2022). Janus Faced Migration Policymaking: A Case Study of Afghan-European Migration Policy. *Refugee Watch*, 60, pp. 13–28.

Hyndman, J. (2012). The Geopolitics of Migration and Mobility. *Geopolitics*, 17(2), pp. 243–255.

Ibrahimi, N. (2017). *The Hazaras and the Afghan State: Rebellion, Exclusion and the Struggle for Recognition*. Oxford, UK: Oxford University Press.

Jubany, O. (2017). *Screening Asylum in a Culture of Disbelief. Truths, Denials and Skeptical Borders*. Cham, Switzerland: Palgrave Macmillan.

Kakar, M. H. (1995). *Afghanistan: The Soviet Invasion and the Afghan Response 1979–1982*. Berkeley: University of California Press.

Khosravi, S. (2018). Stolen Time. *Radical Philosophy*, 2(3), pp. 38–41.

Klaus, F. (2006). *Caravans, Conflicts and Trade in Afghanistan and British India 1800–1980*. Rhodos International Science and Art Publishers, Copenhagen.

Langenkamp, D. (2003). The Victory of Expediency-Afghan Refugees and Pakistan in the 1990s. The Fletcher Forum of World Affairs, 27, p. 229.

Majidi, N. (2018). Community Dimensions of Smuggling: The Case of Afghanistan and Somalia. *The Annals of the American Academy of Political and Social Science*, 676(1), pp. 97–113.

Minority Rights Group International. (2008). *World Directory of Minorities and Indigenous Peoples – Afghanistan: Hazaras*, https://www.refworld.org/reference/ countryrep/mrgi/2008/en/107199 [Accessed 11 Nov. 2024].

Mixed Migration Centre. (2021). *Smuggling and mixed migration: Insights and key messages drawn from a decade of MMC research and 4Mi data collection*. Available at: http://www.mixedmigration.org/

Mohammadi, A., Nimar, R. and Savage, E. (2019). We are the ones they come to when nobody can help: Afghan smugglers' perceptions of themselves and their communities. *Migration Research Series*, No 56, International Organisation for Migration (IOM), Geneva.

Monsutti, A. (2003). HAZĀRA: ii. HISTORY. (Online ed.). https://iranicaonline.org/articles/hazara-2 [Retrieved 25 May 2024].

Monsutti, A. (2005). *War and Migration: Social Networks and Economic Strategies of the Hazaras of Afghanistan*. Routledge.

Monsutti, A. (2008). Afghan Migratory Strategies and the Three Solutions to the Refugee Problem. *Refugee Survey Quarterly*, 27(1), pp. 58–73.

Monsutti, A. (2012). *War and Migration: Social Networks and Economic Strategies of the Hazaras of Afghanistan*. London: Routledge.

Mousavi, S. A. (1998). *The Hazaras of Afghanistan: An Historical, Cultural, Economic and Political Study*. Richmond, Surrey: Curzon Press.

Mousavi, S. A. (2018). *The Hazaras of Afghanistan*. London: Routledge.

Nimkar, R. and Mohammadi, A. (2023). A Widening Moral Rift: The Complex Interactions between EU Externalization and Afghan Border Ecosystems. *The ANNALS of the American Academy of Political and Social Science*, 1(709), pp. 46–64.

Olszewska, Z. (2015). *The Pearl of Dari: Poetry and Personhood among Young Afghans in Iran*. Bloomington, Indiana: Indiana University Press.

Phoenix, A. (2005). Remembered racialization: Young people and positioning in differential understandings. In: K. Murji and J. Solomos, eds., *Racialization: Studies in Theory and Practice*. Oxford, UK: Oxford University Press, pp. 103–122.

Safri, M. (2011). The Transformation of the Afghan Refugee: 1979–2009. *The Middle East Journal*, 65(4), pp. 587–601.

Schuster, L. (2004). *The Use and Abuse of Political Asylum in Britain and Germany*. London: Routledge.

Schuster, L. (2010). Globalization, migration and citizenship. In: P. Hill Collins and J. Solomos, eds., *Handbook of Race and Ethnic Studies*. London: Sage, pp. 332–350.

Schuster, L. (2016). Unmixing migrants and refugees. In: A. Triandafyllidou, ed., *Routledge Handbook of Immigrant and Refugee Studies*. London: Routledge.

Schuster, L. and Majidi, M. (2013). What Happens Post-Deportation? The Experience of Deported Afghans. *Migration Studies,* 1(2), pp. 241–260.

Schuster, L. and Majidi, M. (2014). Deportation Stigma and Re-Migration. *Journal of Ethnic and Migration Studies*. Special Issue: Deportation, Anxiety, Justice: New Ethnographic Perspectives, 4(41), pp. 635–652.

Shamlu, A. (Trans.). (1984). *Siyah hamchon a'maq-e Afrighaye khodam* (Black like the depths of my own Africa). Tehran: Ebtikar.

UNHCR (2024). Annex 2 – Populations protected and / or assisted by UNHCR by country/territory of origin. https://www.unhcr.org/refugee-statistics/insights/annexes/trends-annexes.html?situation=2 [Accessed 27 Nov. 2024].

Van Houte, M., Siegel, M. and Davids, T. (2016). Deconstructing the Meanings of and Motivations for Return: An Afghan Case Study. *Comparative Migration Studies*, 4, pp. 1–17.

Vossughi, F. and Mohseni, M. (2016). Investigation Citizen Attitudes on Foreign Immigrants Resident in Mashhad. *Geographical Research*, 31(2), pp. 4–18.

Recommended watching

Fazili, H. (2018). *Midnight Traveller* (documentary). Old Chilly Pictures

Sahibdad, R. (2006). *Talib* available at: https://www.youtube.com/watch?v=xQqU7pWt0mY

Sahibdad, R. (2017). *Welcome to Paristan* The Kingdom

Index

www.ingramcontent.com/pod-product-compliance
Lightning Source LLC
Chambersburg PA
CBHW070343270326
41926CB00017B/3955